# RAINBOW FOOD

text and photographs by
**Linda Louis**

# RAINBOW FOOD

## 50 RECIPES COLOR-CODED AND VITAMINIZED

FIREFLY BOOKS

# A FIREFLY BOOK

Published by Firefly Books Ltd. 2019
Text and photographs © 2018 Linda Louis
English edition © 2019 Firefly Books Ltd.
First published by Editions GALLIMARD, Paris
© Editions GALLIMARD, collection Alternatives, 2018

First printing

**Library of Congress Control Number:** 2019937138

**Library and Archives Canada Cataloguing in Publication**
Title: Rainbow food : 50 recipes color-coded and vitaminized /
    text and photographs by Linda Louis.
Other titles: Rainbow food. English
Names: Louis, Linda, 1978- author.
Description: Translation of: Rainbow food : 50 recettes
    colorées et vitaminées. | Includes index.
Identifiers: Canadiana 20190087390 |
    ISBN 9780228102243 (softcover)
Subjects: LCSH: Cooking. | LCSH: Cooking (Fruit) | LCSH:
    Cooking (Vegetables) | LCSH: Food—Vitamin content. |
    LCSH: Diet therapy. | LCGFT: Cookbooks.
Classification: LCC TX714 .L6813 2019 | DDC 641.5/63—dc23

Published in Canada by
Firefly Books Ltd.
50 Staples Avenue, Unit 1
Richmond Hill, Ontario
L4B 0A7

Published in the United States by
Firefly Books (U.S.) Inc.
P.O. Box 1338, Ellicott Station
Buffalo, New York
14205

Graphic design: Bigre ! - www.bigre.net

Printed in China

*Thank you to my family, to Laurent and to Madeline,*
*for letting me borrow her pots and pans,*
*and to my occasional and regular tasters and testers.*

*Linda*

# TABLE OF CONTENTS

# TABLE OF CONTENTS

# EAT THE RAINBOW!

*"Eat the Rainbow!" is a good phrase to tell children when they sulk at dinner! This expression underlines both the importance of eating fruits and vegetables as well as eating a variety of differently colored fruits and vegetables. Eating the rainbow also allows you to benefit from a variety of nutrients. That's the whole point of this book: eating better — in a chromotherapeutic way!*

## ENJOY YOURSELF AND COOK POSITIVELY

What a joy it is to fill your basket with beautiful vegetables and colorful fruits, chop them up and present them attractively (cooking can be a great way to whet one's appetite)! Having experienced it myself during gray and rainy winter days, I have no doubt that rainbow foods can put a smile on your face and liven up your dishes with every color of the rainbow, much more so than the monotonous, monochromatic menus that were all the rage in the early 2000s.

## FILLING UP ON ANTIOXIDANTS

Rainbow foods offer nutritional biodiversity in a single dish. Fruits and vegetables, thanks to their varied pigmentations, offer a wide range of antioxidants, such as chlorophyll (green), lutein (yellow), beta-carotene (orange), lycopene (red) and anthocyanins (red, pink, purple, blue). It's perhaps a lucky coincidence, or simply natural alchemy, that many of these pigments also benefit our eyes! No less astonishing is the fact that anthocyanins in red berries (such as black currants, raspberries, pomegranates) are excellent for blood circulation.

## A FUN WAY TO EAT MORE FRUITS AND VEGETABLES

The green-yellow-orange-red-pink-purple-blue equation encourages us to cook with more plants. For instance, in the pickles recipe on page 48, the traditional pickling cucumbers are replaced with Chioggia beets, carrots, radishes and romanesco; a simple tart is transformed into a tutti-frutti version with green rhubarb, yellow cherry plums, red plums and purple blueberries.

## ENCOURAGING PEOPLE TO EAT ETHICALLY

By buying (or indeed growing!) heritage vegetables, known for their wide range of colors (tomatoes and carrots, multicolored peppers and beets, red cabbage, purple cauliflower, purple potatoes...), we deviate from the standards imposed on us by mass distribution and thus promote biodiversity and seed conservation.

## TAKING THE VEGETARIAN PLUNGE

These simple recipes reinvent vegetarian cuisine, often wrongly considered bland and boring. A complete meal of veggies in the style of rainbow foods exudes vitality and encourages even the most skeptical eaters to take the plunge, taste this food, appreciate it and say to themselves: "It's beautiful, it's good, it changes things, so why not?"

Naturally, this collection of colorful and vitamin-packed recipes has nothing to do with the rainbow or "unicorn" foods in which ingredients are simply dyed with food coloring (most of which are allergenic and potentially dangerous to our health). The fluorescent hues on those plasticine-looking cakes are neither appetizing nor nutritionally interesting! That being said, these two culinary trends have common roots in the "rainbow" artistic movement that was inspired by the counterculture of the 1960s as well as the cartoons of the 1980s. All over the world you can see streets, walls, works of art, DIY creations and even people decked out in the colors of the peace flag and LGBT flag. They're thumbing their nose at dullness, pessimism and closed-mindedness... Let's follow that lead and put it on our plates!

# THE COLORS
## OF LIFE

*Why are flowers and fruits colorful? In nature, nothing is trivial. If the pigments in vegetables make them even more beautiful, this is not meant to simply whet the appetite of Homo erectus but to also favor the reproduction of plants and their conquest of propagation across our planet.*

### COLOR, MOTHER NATURE'S SECRET WEAPON OF SEDUCTION

In the same way that bees and other pollinating insects are attracted to colorful flowers, animals, including humans, naturally seek out colorful fruits and vegetables. The objective is the same: nourishment. Color is our first contact, our first sensory experience of food, since we see it before we're able to touch it, feel it, taste it and perhaps even appreciate it. Without color, we would need to go directly to the olfactory stage, as we do when we choose melons whose light green skin gives no indication whatsoever of its flavor. Bright colors are signs of ripeness and edibility (generally), and they encourage the consumption of fruits and thus help spread the seeds they contain. To us, they're the promise of a sweet, juicy and tasty fruit that will provide us with energy and vitamins.

Unripe, small, green, hard, tart and unsweet fruits are rich in tannins, which are chemical compounds that act as the plant's line of defense against overeager fruit eaters. Unripe fruits are thus protected by their color, but also tart flavor. They likely won't be eaten until the seeds inside are ready. As they ripen, the fruits expand, soften and turn yellow, orange, red, pink, purple... This change in color is linked to the gradual destruction of chlorophyll and the accelerated production of pigments. The intense color of the fruits thus becomes a visual sign that indicates they're finally ready to be eaten. At the same time, tannins gradually disappear and sugars increase, making the plants even more appetizing. The fruits have served their purpose: protecting and feeding the seeds with their fleshy and sweet shell, and contributing to their propagation thanks to external agents drawn by their colors and appearance![1]

Conversely, if the fruit is brown or blackened, this dark color will be interpreted as a sign of decomposition, warning us about its potential toxicity. We instinctively reject such fruits to avoid any risk. These phenomena of attraction and rejection of colors are totally unconscious and are based on thousands of years of evolution during which we've learned to recognize what's good for us from what's not.

## THE CULTURAL HERITAGE OF OUR PERCEPTIONS OF COLORS

It should be noted that other factors, such as cultural and societal ones and those related to our personal or collective experience with food, play an undeniable complementary role in our perception of the colors of food. For example, a black hamburger bun hasn't been as successful as expected among Americans, yet it was more appreciated by the Japanese, who are used to eating black foods that are considered nutritious, such as black mushrooms, black garlic, black sesame or nori seaweed. In a study conducted among people who are used to drinking a certain brand of soda, it was noted that if the yellow color on the product packaging was increased by 15%, consumers had the feeling that the taste of their favorite drink was more lemony. The recipe hadn't changed: it was merely the effect of this new packaging on their subconscious, which had tricked their senses!

We are well aware to what extent the colors of foods, but also their environment (packaging, dishes, tablecloths, napkins) can condition our appetite.

---

1 Source: Catherine Lenne, Dans la peau d'une plante: 70 questions impertinentes sur la vie secrète des plantes (Paris, France: Éditions Belin, 2014).

# PLANT PIGMENTS
## AND THEIR INFLUENCE ON
# OUR HEALTH

*Nature is perfectly formed: once they've seduced us visually, these amazing pigments act as a kind of preservative in our bodies. They counter the negative effects of aging, overly rich diets and certain types of pollution.*

The oxygen in your body doesn't always transform itself properly, and it can produce what are called free radicals. These are very reactive and can attack our cells in order to stabilize themselves. In doing so, they can oxidize these cells and age them prematurely. In order to combat these effects, our body has natural detoxifying systems: vitamins A, C and E as well as natural pigments, which play an antioxidant role in our bodies. Here are the main ones:[1]

## CHLOROPHYLL

This pigment is found in all green vegetables. It's fat soluble and blends well with oil but not very well with water. Green foods are rich in iron, folic acid and vitamins A, C and E.

Asparagus, avocados, cabbages (broccoli, Brussels sprouts, kale), zucchini, spinach, aromatic herbs, kiwifruits, rhubarb, matcha green tea, green tomatoes, lettuce.[2]

> ### Benefits[3]
> • Antioxidant properties
> • Helps blood regenerate and wounds heal
> • Cleans and protects gut flora and the liver
> • Lowers cholesterol

[1] This is only a partial list.

[2] Every plant contains many pigments, which give it a unique color.

[3] The qualities listed below, even when cited and proven by scientific studies and published in scientific journals, are for information purposes only and do not constitute a medical prescription.

- Stimulates estrogen production and thereby reduces the risk of ovarian cysts, vaginal infections and irregular periods
- Boosts the immune system
- Maintains the acid-base balance
- Sanitizes the mouth

## CAROTENOIDS

**Beta-carotene (or provitamin A):** an orange pigment (from the carotene family) that is fat soluble, found in many fruits and vegetables and a precursor to vitamin A (or retinol). It's also visible on dead leaves in the fall, when chlorophyll disappears due to the lower light levels and colder temperatures. In order to optimize your intake of the beta-carotene from the plants you consume, add a bit of fat to your recipes (e.g., carrot juice with colza oil, an apricot smoothie with almond butter, sweet potato mash prepared with coconut oil). It is worth noting that while beta-carotene degrades slightly when cooked, it degrades more so through oxidation. Keep fruits and vegetables in a cool, dry place, away from direct sunlight.

Carrots, squashes, sweet potatoes, orange tomatoes, red and orange peppers, apricots, melons, oranges, peaches, but also certain green vegetables: broccoli, spinach, parsley, dandelion (the orange color is concealed by the green of the chlorophyll)

Benefits:
- Helps visual acuity (particularly night vision) and prevents macular degeneration
- Reduces the risk of breast cancer and cataracts
- Contributes to the growth of bones and teeth
- Promotes healthy skin and mucosa
- Protects from external aggressors (e.g., the sun)
- Involved in the proper functioning of the immune system
- Helps iron absorption

**Beta-cryptoxanthin:** an orange pigment that is found in persimmons, pumpkins, red peppers, goji berries and papayas and has nutritional and therapeutic benefits that are akin to beta-carotene.

**Lycopene:** a red pigment (from the carotene family) that is mostly found in tomatoes. Cooking concentrates the available amount of lycopene. Coulis, ketchup and tomato paste are therefore naturally rich in this substance.

Red peppers, tomatoes, goji berries, guavas, persimmons, papayas, watermelons, pink grapefruit

Benefits:
- Protects blood vessels and may limit the risks of cardiovascular diseases, such as arterioslerosis (the loss of arterial elasticity due to sclerosis, which is caused by the accumulation of harmful cholesterol, called LDL)
- May help prevent prostate cancer

**Xanthophylls:** yellow pigments (from the carotene family) that are found in green plants as well as yellow ones (in green plants, the yellow is concealed by the green of the chlorophyll). Lutein and zeaxanthin are the most well-known xanthophylls, due to their benefits for the retina and its central part, called the *macula lutea*. Both lutein and zeaxanthin are essential to filter UV rays and blue light, thereby neutralizing the free radicals generated by the sun's rays. You can eat mango with coconut milk or spinach and green pepper with olive oil to help absorption. And let's not forget crocetin (saffron), canthaxanthin (chanterelles) and astaxanthin (seaweed, plankton, shrimp, salmon).

Lutein: avocados, broccoli, kale, yellow zucchini, spinach, peas, green peppers, marigolds, pineapples, kiwifruits, mandarins, mangos, oranges, pistachio nuts

Zeaxanthin: corn, orange peppers

Benefits:
- Limits macular degeneration linked to aging and the risk of cataracts

## POLYPHENOLS

**Anthocyanins:** red, pink, blue and purple pigments that are known for their strong antioxidant properties. In the ORAC (Oxygen Radical Absorbance Capacity) index, which helps assess the antioxidant properties of food, red plants are at the top of the list of fruits and vegetables that significantly combat free radicals. They're water soluble, and the color varies depending on the degree of acidity or basicity. In combination with carotenes, these pigments also give leaves their characteristic red/orange colors in the fall, when the chlorophyll breaks down, revealing the pigments that were hidden underneath.

Artichokes, eggplants, red beets, red Swiss chard, red cabbage, red onions, olives, purple sweet potatoes, red peppers, blue potatoes, pink radishes, açai berries, cranberries, black chokeberries, black currants, cherries, strawberries, raspberries, pomegranates, red currants, blackberries, blueberries, blood oranges, red grapes, elderberries

**Benefits:**
- Anti-inflammatory and antibacterial properties
- Lowers harmful LDL cholesterol and increases the healthy cholesterols
- Protects blood vessels and may lower the risks of vascular diseases

**Flavonoids:** these are the most important category of polyphenols and include quercetin (considered the most antioxidant flavonoid) and condensed tannins such as procyanidin.
Quercetin: capers, lovage, yellow and red onions, black currants, apples, black elderberries, dark chocolate, black tea, green tea, red wine
Procyanidin: red wine, walnuts

**Benefits:**
- Antioxidant and anti-inflammatory properties
- Reduces the risk of allergies
- Strengthens small blood vessels and may reduce the risks of cardiovascular disease

**Curcumin:** an intense yellow pigment found in turmeric, which is a root from Southeast Asia. Since it's fat soluble, it must be mixed with fat (e.g., ghee, coconut oil) for your body to be able to absorb it. Studies have shown that piperine, an active substance found in black pepper, increases its bioavailability. It is worth noting that turmeric may turn deep red in an alkaline environment (e.g., in a cake batter that includes baking powder or baking soda).

**Benefits:**
- Strong antioxidant and anti-inflammatory properties
- Helps relieve problems associated with digestion, the stomach, the liver and the skin (such as eczema)
- Helps relieve rheumatoid pain, muscle aches and tooth aches
- Stimulates the immune system
- May reduce the risk of cancer (particularly breast cancer and cancers of the aerodigestive tract)

## BETALAINS

**Betanin:** a pigment that ranges from yellow to reddish purple and is most notably found in beets. Its name is derived from the beet's scientific name, *Beta vulgaris*.
Beets, prickly pears, red dragon fruit

**Benefits:**
- Strong antioxidant properties
- Helps protect the liver and cardiovascular system
- May help prevent certain cancers (skin, liver and lung)

## PHYCOCYANIN

This is a combination of proteins and pigments that contributes to the photosynthesis of spirulina and gives it its bluish-green color.

**Benefits:**
- Strengthens the immune system
- Stimulates blood production
- Helps prevent hypertension
- Plays an anti-inflammatory and antioxidant role in the body

## PIGMENTS AND MORE!

These foods, however, contain more than just antioxidant pigments. They also have a range of vitamins, minerals and nutrients that are essential to our organism. First of all, most fruits and vegetables are rich in fiber, which is essential to bowel function. Then there is vitamin C, which has strong antioxidant properties and is found in green vegetables, citrus fruits and red berries; vitamin E, which is found in spinach, mangos, dried fruits and canned or preserved tomatoes; folic acid (vitamin B9), vitamin K, iron and calcium, which are found in green vegetables; and magnesium and potassium, which are found in vegetables and dried fruits.

# EAT THE RAINBOW !

*Eat the rainbow, and reap the benefits of antioxidants!*

ALTERN ATIVES

## RED

**Lycopene** (carotenes): found mostly in tomatoes; protects blood vessels and helps prevent cardiovascular diseases
*Red peppers, tomatoes (sauces), goji berries, guavas, persimmons, papaya, watermelons, pink grapefruit*
**Anthocyanins** (polyphenols): antioxidants renowned for their antibacterial and anti-inflammatory properties
*Red carrots, red onions, red kidney beans, cherries, strawberries, raspberries, blood oranges, red apples, red pears*

## WHITE

**Potassium:** essential for the nervous system and the proper function of muscles and the kidneys
**Sulfur compounds:** known for their antifungal and antibacterial properties
*Garlic, celery, cauliflower, endives, white beans, onions, turnips, parsnips, potatoes, black radishes, salsifies, Jerusalem artichokes, bananas*

## ORANGE

**Beta-carotene, beta-cryptoxanthin** (carotenes): benefit the eyes, bones and skin
*Carrots, squashes, sweet potatoes, orange tomatoes, red and orange peppers, apricots, goji berries, persimmons, melons, cherry plums, oranges, papayas, peaches, and green plants such as broccoli, spinach, parsley, dandelion*

## PINK

**Betalain:** helps protect the liver and cardiovascular system
*Beets, prickly pears, red dragon fruit*

## PURPLE

**Anthocyanins** (polyphenols): antioxidants renowned for their antibacterial and anti-inflammatory properties
*Purple artichokes, eggplants, carrots, sweet potatoes, purple potatoes, red cabbage, olives, black rice, açai berries, black chokeberries, black currants, black figs, blackberries, blueberries, damson plums, red grapes, elderberries, red wine*

## GREEN

**Chlorophyll:** a cleansing substance that acts on the blood, gut flora, liver and female sphere
*Green asparagus, celery, cabbage, cucumbers, zucchini, spinach, herbs, kiwifruits, rhubarb, matcha green tea, lettuce, spirulina*

## YELLOW

**Lutein and zeaxanthin** (carotenes): renowned for their benefits to the eye
**Curcumin** (polyphenol): found in turmeric, it is known for its antioxidant and anti-inflammatory properties
*Avocado, yellow zucchini, turmeric, corn, yellow peppers, oranges, pineapples, mangos, pistachio nuts, as well as broccoli, kale, spinach, peas, kiwifruits*

# HOMEMADE NATURAL
# FOOD COLORINGS

*Food colorings are especially useful for sweet recipes (see page 89). You will find a few organic powdered colorings based on spinach, turmeric, tomatoes or beets in stores, but if you feel like going for it, here are a few quick and easy techniques to make natural food colorings... all packed with vitamins!*

## •UNSWEETENED POWDERED FOOD COLORING

*1/3 cup (75 ml) tomato paste (orange), finely diced beets (pink), currants (raspberry red), chopped spinach (green)... (whatever you choose)*

**1.** Blend the fruits or vegetables (except for the tomato paste) until you have a very smooth puree.
**2.** Spread the puree on a tray covered with parchment paper and leave to dry in a dehydrator (or oven) at 120°F (50°C) for 2 ½ hours (slightly less for tomato paste). The layer will then become dry and brittle.
**3.** Blend the dry pieces, and store the powder in an airtight jar.

## •COLORED SUGARS

*1/2 cup (125 ml) colorful fruit or vegetable juice (beet, carrot, tomato, red currant, blueberry, etc.), 1 cup (250 ml) turbinado (or raw) sugar*

**1.** Reduce the juice by half in a saucepan over low heat, until it becomes a light syrup.
**2.** Add the sugar and mix well.
**3.** Leave to dry, if necessary, at 120°F (50°C), on a tray covered with parchment paper.

## •CONCENTRATED FRUIT PULP COLORINGS

*3 ½ cups (875 ml) apricots, chopped mango, strawberries, raspberries, blueberries, black currants or 2 cups (500 ml) purple grape juice, 1/4 cup (60 ml) turbinado (or raw) sugar, the juice of 1 lemon*

**1.** Blend the fruits and strain them to remove the peel and seeds.
**2.** Pour the resulting pulp into a saucepan and add the sugar and a splash of lemon juice.
**3.** Heat the mixture over very low heat for 30 minutes (or longer, depending on the amount of liquid in the mixture), stirring occasionally to prevent it from sticking to the bottom of the pan.
**4.** Near the end of cooking, you should have a thick, concentrated pulp (be careful, as microdrops of concentrate can splatter and may burn your hands, so wear gloves if needed).
**5.** Pour into a canning jar, such as a Mason jar (around 8 oz. [250 ml]).

## •HOMEMADE FRUIT OR VEGETABLE JUICE

In certain recipes, you will need fruit or vegetable juices to color ingredients (particularly blueberry and spinach juice). You can buy them ready-made at an organic supermarket or make them yourself.

**1.** Juice the fruits and vegetables (carrots, blueberries, pomegranates, spinach, etc.) in a juicer.
**2.** If you don't have a juicer, blend them with a splash of water, and then pass the pulp through a strainer, pressing firmly to extract as much juice as possible.
**3.** Refrigerate in small bottles (or the juices can be frozen).

# APPETIZERS

*Let's get this recipe collection off to a festive start, with a good appetizer made of well-seasoned vegetable spreads, vegetable sticks, olives and crackers. Be sure to present everything beautifully on your table and delight in your guests' stunned expressions!*

# DIPS AND SPREADS

### • CHICKPEA/PEA HUMMUS

FOR 4 PEOPLE · PREPARATION: 10 MIN · STORAGE: 3 DAYS

**INGREDIENTS** 1 cup (250 ml) of cooked chickpeas (or peas, steamed for 20 minutes) • 1 tbsp. (15 ml) tahini or sesame butter (or cashew butter) • 2 cloves garlic, peeled • ⅓ cup (75 ml) olive oil • ¼ cup (60 ml) lemon juice • salt • freshly ground pepper

**1.** Blend the still-warm chickpeas (or peas) with the tahini and garlic.

**2.** Once the ingredients are well combined, add the olive oil, lemon juice, salt and pepper.

**3.** For a smoother texture, you can pass the hummus through a sieve. Taste and adjust the seasoning, if necessary.

### • TOMATO OR GREEN OLIVE DIP

FOR 4 PEOPLE · PREPARATION: 5 MIN · STORAGE: 3 DAYS

**INGREDIENTS** 4 oz. (100 g) silken tofu • ½ cup (125 ml) sun-dried tomatoes in oil and 1 pinch red pepper flakes or ½ cup (125 ml) pitted green olives and 1 tsp. (5 ml) marjoram.

**1.** Blend all ingredients until you have a smooth texture.

### • TZATZIKI

FOR 4 PEOPLE · PREPARATION: 15 MIN · REST: 1 ½ H · STORAGE: 2 DAYS

**INGREDIENTS** about ½ cucumber • salt • 1 small clove garlic • 4 sprigs dill • 4 mint leaves • ¾ cup (175 ml) Greek yogurt (sheep's milk yogurt, drained in cheesecloth for 3 hours) • salt and pepper

**1.** Wash the cucumber and peel every other strip along the length, to leave a bit of skin. Grate using a large-hole grater. Sprinkle with salt and leave to drain in a strainer for 30 minutes. Squeeze the cucumbers to remove as much liquid as possible.

**2.** Peel the garlic and grate it finely. Wash the herbs and chop finely.

**3.** Whisk the yogurt, and add the garlic, herbs, salt and pepper. Refrigerate for at least 1 hour before serving.

**Accompaniments:** crackers, breadsticks, pita bread cut into triangles, carrot and radish sticks, cherry tomatoes, halved mini peppers, olives, sprouts, etc.

*There are organic food stores that sell snacks made from nuts and dried fruits, which have colors that immediately catch your eye.*
*I suggest making your own mix with dried pineapple and golden berries, goji berries, peanuts, hazelnuts, pistachio nuts and pumpkin and poppy seeds. A snack that will be enjoyed by young and old alike!*

# TRAIL MIX

FOR 4 PEOPLE · PREPARATION: 5 MIN · COOKING TIME: 6–7 MIN · STORAGE: 1 MONTH

**INGREDIENTS**

2 tbsp. (30 ml) pumpkin seeds • 2 tbsp. (30 ml) shelled pistachio nuts • 4 slices dried pineapple
• 3 tbsp. (45 ml) peanuts • 3 tbsp. (45 ml) dried golden berries • 2 tbsp. (30 ml) goji berries
• 2 tbsp. (30 ml) whole hazelnuts • 1 tbsp. (15 ml) poppy seeds • gray salt

**1.** Combine the pumpkin seeds, pistachio nuts, peanuts, golden berries, goji berries and poppy seeds in a large bowl.

**2.** Cut the pineapple into small triangles with a pair of scissors. Add it to the bowl.

**3.** Toast the hazelnuts in a pan over medium heat for 6 to 7 minutes, and then add them to the bowl, with the rest of the ingredients.

**4.** Salt to taste, stir to combine and serve. Store any leftovers in an airtight jar.

**Note:** you can make a color gradient by arranging each ingredient on a plate, as shown in the photo opposite, or combine all of the ingredients together in a bowl.

*This light appetizer is vitamin packed and, of course, colorful! Carrots, radishes and beets have all met up in Italy for a carpaccio and a little gremolata presented with carrot tops rather than parsley. This is a dynamic crudités platter that is sure to whet everyone's appetite.*

# ROOT VEGETABLE CARPACCIO WITH GREMOLATA

**FOR 4 PEOPLE · PREPARATION: 30 MIN · REST: 2 H · STORAGE: 2 DAYS**

......................................................................................................................................

### INGREDIENTS

*Carpaccio:* 1 small black radish • 1 white carrot • 1 gold ball turnip • 1 orange carrot • 4 pink radishes • 1 small red beet • 1 small Chioggia beet (with pink and white stripes) • 1 red meat (or watermelon) radish • gray salt • drizzle olive oil • sesame seeds to garnish

*Gremolata:* zest and juice of 1 lemon • zest of 1 orange • 2 cloves garlic, germ removed • tenderest and lightest tops from 1 carrot • ¼ cup (60 ml) olive oil • salt • freshly ground pepper

**1.** Carefully wash the vegetables under running water, using a brush. Peel the turnip, beets and red meat radishes, but not the other vegetables.

**2.** Slice them very finely using a mandoline slicer, as you would to make potato chips.

**3.** Place the slices neatly on a platter or on four individual plates. Season with salt* and a drizzle of olive oil, and leave to marinate in the fridge for two hours.

**4.** Prepare the gremolata by crushing the citrus zest, garlic and carrot tops with a mortar and pestle, gradually adding the olive oil and lemon juice. Add salt and pepper to taste, adjusting the seasoning as desired.

**5.** Serve the carpaccio with the sauce and grilled bread.

**\*Good to know:** salting the vegetables in a marinade helps to make them more tender.

*The concept is simple: make a vegan cheese with almonds and lacto-fermented tamarind-flavored tofu, and color it with vegetables. The result is a creamy, aromatic spread that beautifully tints slices of sandwich bread. Have fun cutting vegetables with star- or heart-shaped cookie cutters and garnishing with poppy or sesame seeds. Children will devour these fairylike sandwiches in a heartbeat!*

# SOY CHEESE OPEN-FACED SANDWICHES

FOR 4–9 PEOPLE · PREPARATION: 1H · REST: 4 H + 2 H · STORAGE: 1 DAY (FOR THE SANDWICHES) 3 DAYS (FOR THE CHEESE)

## INGREDIENTS

1 ½ cups (375 ml) blanched almonds • 7 oz. (200 g) tamarind-flavored fermented tofu • 1 clove garlic, crushed • 3 tbsp. (45 ml) lemon juice • ½ cup (125 ml) baby spinach leaves
• ½ cup (125 ml) cubed red kuri squash, roasted with 1 pinch turmeric • ½ small beet, cooked
• 3 tbsp. (45 ml) black currant preserves • salt • black pepper

*Toppings:* Chioggia beets • yellow beets • avocado (+ lemon juice) • corn • sprouts • spinach leaves • cherry tomatoes • golden, brown or black sesame seeds • poppy seeds • sandwich bread

**1.** Soak the almonds for 4 hours. Rinse well and blend with the tofu, garlic and lemon juice until you have a smooth paste.

**2.** Divide the cheese in four and blend each section with a different ingredient: spinach, red kuri squash, beets or black currants. Salt and pepper to taste, and adjust seasoning as needed. Chill the cheese.

**3.** Prepare the beets for the topping: finely shred using a mandolin slicer, and cut out stars using a shaped cookie cutter.

**4.** Prepare the avocado: slice it in two, and carefully peel each half. Slice it finely and squeeze a little lemon juice over the slices, to keep them from browning.

**5.** Halve the cherry tomatoes.

**6.** Spread a little colored cheese on each slice of bread. Add toppings as shown in the photo opposite. Serve immediately.

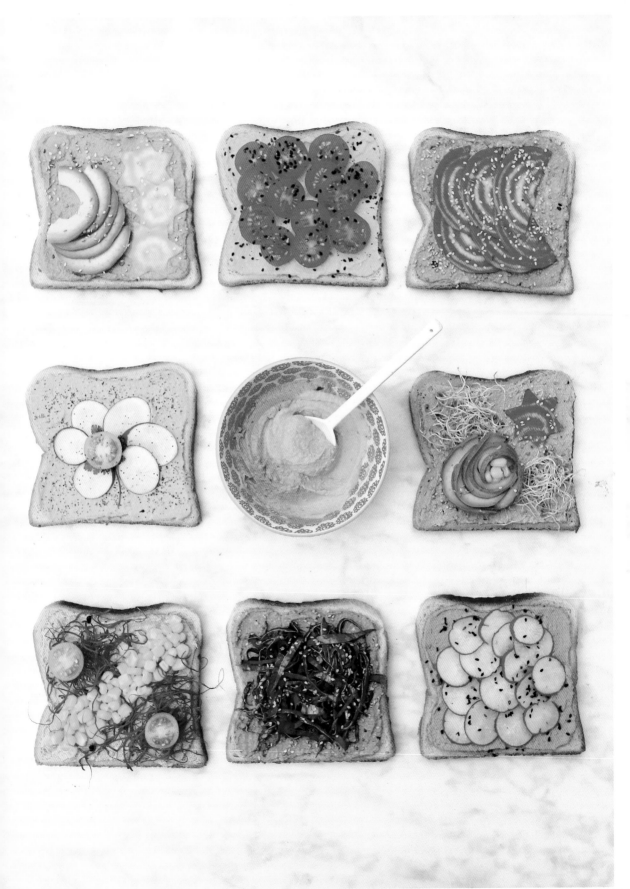

*Tomatoes aren't the only vegetable in the nightshade family that comes in a thousand colors! Their cousin, the bell pepper, dons yellow, orange, red, green and even purple shades, depending on the variety. Grilling them under the broiler — or on embers — softens their flesh, concentrates their aromas, develops a deliciously sweet flavor and doesn't alter their color at all, with the exception of purple ones, which turn a bit more blue. Like red cabbage, purple peppers contain anthocyanins, which are natural pigments that change color based on the acidity/basicity of their environment. Just basting them with the lemon juice in the marinade will restore their lovely purple tint.*

# MARINATED GRILLED PEPPERS

FOR 4 PEOPLE · PREPARATION: 45 MIN · COOKING: 20–30 MIN · STORAGE: 3 DAYS

**INGREDIENTS**

1 purple pepper • 1 green pepper • 1 yellow pepper • 1 orange pepper
• 1 red pepper (all peppers should be of similar size) • 1 small clove garlic • 1 pinch salt • freshly ground pepper
• ⅓ cup (75 ml) olive oil • 3 tbsp. (45 ml) lemon juice

**1.** Preheat oven on the broiler setting (around 460°F [240°C]). Chop the peppers lengthwise into quarters. Remove the stems and seeds and discard. Rinse the quarters of pepper.

**2.** Arrange them skin-side up on a sheet pan. Broil for 20 to 30 minutes, until the skin is slightly blackened and the flesh has become more tender (check on them as they cook, to make sure they don't get too soft).

**3.** Place the cooked peppers in a large bowl and cover with a plate. Leave to cool for 15 minutes.

**4.** Carefully peel the skin from the peppers, and then chop the flesh into thin ½-inch (1 cm) strips.

**5.** Arrange them on a rectangular serving platter, forming a rainbow.

**6.** Peel and mince the garlic. Combine with the olive oil and lemon juice. Add salt and pepper, and then pour the marinade over the peppers.

**7.** Chill for 30 minutes before enjoying the peppers with some grilled bread, fresh cheese, tabbouleh or whatever accompaniments you like.

*Did you know the cabbage family isn't just limited to regular cabbage, Brussels sprouts and bok choy? Beautiful flowering vegetables like broccoli, cauliflower and romanesco are also part of the Brassica genus. I thought these colorful florets would be as good to look at as they would be to eat. Mixed with couscous, shallots and pomegranate seeds, they make an excellent tabbouleh!*

# COLORED CABBAGE TABBOULEH

FOR 4 PEOPLE · PREPARATION: 25 MIN · REST: 5 MIN · COOKING: 1 MIN · STORAGE: 2 DAYS

### INGREDIENTS

½ cup (125 ml) couscous · 2 florets romanesco · 1 floret broccoli · 3 florets purple cauliflower · 3 florets white cauliflower · ½ pomegranate · 2 shallots · ⅓ cup (75 ml) olive oil · 3 tbsp. (45 ml) lemon juice · salt and freshly ground pepper

**1.** Place the couscous in a bowl along with a pinch of salt and a drizzle of olive oil. Bring ⅓ cup + 1 tbsp. (90 ml) of water to a boil, and then pour over the couscous. Stir to combine, and then cover with a plate and leave to stand for 5 minutes.

**2.** Separate the cooked couscous with a fork and leave to cool while preparing the other ingredients.

**3.** Wash the cauliflowers, romanesco and broccoli and grate them finely.

**4.** Remove the seeds from the pomegranate.*

**5.** Peel and finely chop the shallots.

**6.** Add all of these ingredients to the couscous. Drizzle with olive oil and lemon juice. Season with salt and pepper to taste, and stir to combine. Taste and adjust seasoning as needed.

**\*Tip:** to easily remove the seeds from the pomegranate, cut the fruit into quarters and dunk them into a bowl of cold water. Expel the seeds while keeping the fruit underwater, to prevent juice from splashing and staining. Discard the peel and white membrane. Strain the seeds.

*Why always have mixed salads? It is so much prettier to stack vegetables, fruits and grains in multicolored layers! That's the principle behind salad in a jar. You can adapt the concept and create salads in glasses, as shown here. Success guaranteed!*

# SALAD IN A GLASS

FOR 4 GLASSES · PREPARATION: 25 MIN · REST: 5 MIN · COOKING: 1 MIN · STORAGE: 2 DAYS

### INGREDIENTS

⅛ red cabbage • 1 small beet, cooked • 1 small red pomegranate • 1 orange carrot • 1 yellow carrot • 6 or 7 florets romanesco • 1 handful leek sprouts • sprigs chervil (to garnish) • salt • black pepper • ¼ cup (60 ml) balsamic vinegar • ⅔ cup (150 ml) olive oil • 1 tsp. (5 ml) soy sauce • 1 rounded tsp. (6 ml) whole-grain mustard

**1.** Finely slice the red cabbage. Salt lightly to soften it. Set aside.

**2.** Finely dice the beet (1/8-inch [3 mm] cubes).

**3.** Remove the seeds from the pomegranate.*

**4.** Peel and coarsely grate the orange and yellow carrots.

**5.** Finely chop the romanesco.

**6.** Layer the salad in glasses, starting with the red cabbage and ending with the sprouts.

**7.** Leave the glasses to chill in the fridge. While the salads chill, make the vinaigrette by blending the balsamic vinegar, olive oil, soy sauce and mustard. Serve with the salads.

**\*Tip:** to easily remove the seeds from the pomegranate, cut the fruit into quarters and dunk them into a bowl of cold water. Expel the seeds while keeping the fruit underwater to prevent juice from splashing and staining. Discard the peel and white membrane. Strain the seeds.

*Would you like to bite into a rainbow? That's what I'm offering you with these spring roll recipes. In the first version, we overlap layers of colored veggies, revealing the color gradient once we take a bite. In the second version, we focus on the exterior of the roll, taking advantage of the transparency of the rice sheets and presenting harmonious slices of avocado and radish or beet spaghetti created with a spiralizer.*

# SPRING ROLLS

## • VERSION 1

**FOR 4–8 PEOPLE** · PREPARATION: 1 H · COOKING: 10 MIN · STORAGE: 3 DAYS

**INGREDIENTS**

½ red cabbage • 2 pinches baking soda • 1 cup (250 ml) baby spinach leaves • 1 large yellow carrot • 1 large orange carrot • 1 Chioggia beet • 8 large sheets rice paper • salt

*Mustard sauce:* ¾ cup (175 ml) vegan hazelnut butter • 1 rounded tbsp. (17 ml) whole-grain mustard • ¼ cup (60 ml) cider vinegar • salt and black pepper

**1.** Finely slice the red cabbage. Cook half in 2 cups (500 ml) water in a covered saucepan for 10 minutes. Drain. The cabbage will have turned blue. To set the color, sprinkle a little baking soda on top.

**2.** Put the other half of the cabbage in a large bowl. Salt lightly, mix well and sit.

**3.** Wash the spinach leaves and leave to dry on a dish towel.

**4.** Peel the carrots and beets. Grate them separately with a large-hole grater.

**5.** Moisten a sheet of rice paper. Leaving a 2-inch (5 cm) space along the bottom and 1-inch (3 cm) spaces at the left and right (see photo on page 40), arrange the vegetables on the sheet in the following order: blue cabbage, reddish purple cabbage, spinach, yellow carrot, orange carrot and, finally, Chioggia beet. Fold the bottom of the sheet over the vegetables, and then fold in the left side then the right. Finally, roll up, creating a tight roll. Wrap in plastic wrap.

**6.** Follow the same procedure with the remaining vegetables and sheets of rice paper, and leave to chill in the fridge.

**7.** Blend the hazelnut butter with the mustard, vinegar and a pinch of salt and pepper. Serve with the spring rolls.

# SPRING ROLLS CONTINUED

## • VERSION 2

FOR 4 PEOPLE · PREPARATION: 40 MIN · REST: 5 MIN · COOKING: 1 MIN · STORAGE: 2 DAYS

### INGREDIENTS

*Topping:* 1 package buckwheat noodles • 1 small head lettuce
• 1 package sprouts (mung bean, sunflower, alfalfa, leek...) • 2 strawberries • ¼ red cabbage • 1 orange carrot
• 1 yellow beet • 1 Chioggia beet • 4 pink radishes • 1 avocado • juice from ½ lemon • ½ cucumber • 1 kiwifruit
• mint leaves • 1 handful crushed peanuts • 12 medium-sized sheets rice paper

*Sweet and sour mango sauce:* ¼ mango • 3 tbsp. (45 ml) lemon juice • 3 tbsp. (45 ml) coconut milk
• 1 tbsp. (15 ml) soy sauce • 1 pinch cayenne pepper

**1.** Cook the noodles in a pot of salted boiling water for 3 minutes. Strain and leave to cool.

**2.** Wash and dry the lettuce. Cut into 1/2 inch (1 cm) strips.

**3.** Slice the strawberries.

**4.** Finely slice the red cabbage. Salt lightly, mix well and let rest.

**5.** Peel the carrot and yellow beet. Grate each with a large-hole grater or slice with a spiralizer (to create vegetable "spaghetti"). Leave some of the carrot and beet in thin discs.

**6.** Slice the Chioggia beet finely using a mandoline slicer.

**7.** Peel the avocado, slice it and drizzle with lemon juice.

**8.** Wash the cucumber and slice it finely using a mandoline slicer. Peel and finely slice the kiwifruit.

**9.** Moisten the first sheet of rice paper. Leaving a 2-inch (5 cm) space along the bottom and 1-inch (3 cm) spaces at the left and right (see photo on page 40), arrange the vegetables on the sheet in the following order: lettuce, buckwheat noodles, sprouts, peanuts.
Top with: 3 fine slices of Chioggia beet and a little red cabbage; or 2 or 3 slices of kiwifruit and cucumber; or a few slices of avocado slices and a little red cabbage; or a few slices of carrot and radish; or 4 or 5 Thai mint leaves and a little grated yellow beet;

# SPRING ROLLS CONTINUED

or a little red cabbage and a few slices of radish; or slices of strawberry and a few leek sprouts; or slices of yellow beet and grated orange carrots.
Fold the bottom of the sheet over the vegetables, and then fold in the left and right sides. Roll up, creating a tight roll. Wrap in plastic wrap. Follow the same procedure for every roll.

**11.** Chill the finished spring rolls.

**12.** Make the sauce by blending the mango, lemon juice, coconut milk, soy sauce and Cayenne pepper.

**Good to know:** if you don't eat these spring rolls right away, keep them in an airtight container to keep them from drying out.

*Served with a little smooth cheese, guacamole or dip (see page 22), these small, savory waffles will bring new fans to your table! In recipes such as this, which require adding fruit/vegetable juices or purees, you should only use white ingredients (flour, milk) to obtain true colors, and leave out the eggs (which are yellow). All the better, as the waffles will be lighter!*

# SAVORY WAFFLES

**FOR 6–8 PEOPLE · PREPARATION: 1 1/2 H · REST: 30 MIN · COOKING: 40 MIN · STORAGE: 3 DAYS**

## INGREDIENTS

*Green waffles:* 1 cup (250 ml) all-purpose flour • 1 rounded tsp. (6 ml) cornstarch • 1 tsp. (5 ml) baking powder • 1 pinch salt • ½ cup (125 ml) soy milk • 4 tsp. (20 ml) sunflower oil • ¼ cup (60 ml) spinach leaves

*Yellow waffles:* ½ cup (125 ml) all-purpose flour • ⅓ cup (75 ml) cornmeal • 1 rounded tsp. (6 ml) cornstarch • 1 tsp. (10 ml) baking powder • 1 pinch salt • ⅔ cup (150 ml) soy milk • 4 tsp. (20 ml) sunflower oil

*Orange waffles:* 1 cup (250 ml) all-purpose flour • 1 rounded tsp. (6 ml) cornstarch • 1 tsp. baking powder • 1 pinch salt • ½ cup (125 ml) soy milk • 4 tsp. (20 ml) sunflower oil • 2 tbsp. (30 ml) tomato paste

*Pink waffles:* 1 cup (250 ml) all-purpose flour • 1 rounded tsp. (6 ml) cornstarch • 1 tsp. (5 ml) baking powder • 1 pinch salt • ½ cup (125 ml) soy milk • 4 tsp. (20 ml) sunflower oil • 3 tbsp. (45 ml) beet juice (or ½ a small beet, blended)

*Purple waffles:* 1 cup (250 ml) all-purpose flour • 1 rounded tsp. (6 ml) cornstarch • 1 tsp. (5 ml) baking powder • 1 pinch salt • ½ cup (125 ml) soy milk • 4 tsp. (20 ml) sunflower oil • 2 tbsp. (30 ml) blueberry juice

**1.** For each kind of batter, mix the flour(s), cornstarch, baking powder and salt together in a bowl. Make a well in the middle of the dry ingredients and add the soy milk, sunflower oil and relevant coloring juice. To make the green waffles, blend the spinach leaves with the sunflower oil and soy milk. Leave the batters to rest for 30 minutes.

**2.** Preheat your waffle maker. When the appliance is hot, oil both sides using a brush. Pour a ladleful of batter onto the cooking surface, according to your waffle makers instructions.

**3.** Close the appliance and leave the waffle to cook for a few minutes (times vary by appliance).

**4.** Carefully unmold the waffles. Follow the same method with the rest of the batters. If you've got leftover batter, make multicolored waffles!

*The galactic effect of these eggs will wow kids and adults alike! The concept is simple and inspired by the famous recipe for tea eggs, which are marbled using black tea. We make hard-boiled eggs, break the shell without peeling them and soak them in a colored juice made with spinach, beets, red cabbage or turmeric powder. The turmeric is also mixed with soy milk rather than water, since it's fat soluble (see page 15).*

# MARBLED EGGS

**FOR 6 EGGS · PREPARATION: 30 MIN · REST: 4 H · COOKING: 10 MIN · STORAGE: 2 DAYS**

............................................................................................................

**INGREDIENTS**

6 eggs
• ½ cup (125 ml) spinach juice (green)
• ½ cup (125 ml) soy milk + 1 tsp. (5 ml) turmeric (yellow)
• ⅓ cup + (75 ml) water + 2 tbsp. (30 ml) beet juice + ½ tsp. (2 ml) turmeric (orange)
• ½ cup (125 ml) beet juice (pink)
• ½ cup (125 ml) red cabbage juice (see recipe on page 134) + a few drops lemon juice (purple)
• ½ cup (125 ml) purple cabbage juice + 1 pinch baking soda (blue)

**1.** Bring a saucepan of water to a boil. Lower the heat and carefully immerse the eggs. Leave them to simmer for 10 minutes.

**2.** In the meantime, pour the colored juices into glasses or small bowls.

**3.** Drain the eggs. Break the shells without peeling them, by hitting them gently and rolling them on a flat surface.

**4.** Place each egg into one of the colored juices. Chill in the fridge for at least 4 hours.

**5.** Peel the eggs to reveal the pretty marbled patterns. If the egg dyed in the purple juice has turned a bit blue, dip it in water with a little lemon juice, and this will restore the purple color.
In all cases, remove the shells at the last minute, right before serving. Otherwise, the marbled patterns tend to fade (except for the turmeric/yellow).

**6.** Try the eggs with guacamole, hummus, tomato-based dips (see recipes on page 22) or crudités.

**Good to know:** leave a small part of the white visible on each egg, to help you control the progression of the color. For example, spinach juice colors less intensely than the other pigments, so don't hesitate to leave that egg in the mixture for a bit longer.

*You can create a jar that ranges from dark pink to yellow (in which case you should only use a little beet, to avoid dyeing the other vegetables) or opt for a preparation that's entirely pink, orange, green or yellow — it's up to you and the veggies you have available. Delicately sour, rich in nutrients and easy to digest, lacto-fermented vegetables are just as enjoyable as classic pickles. You can use them in salads, on cheese sandwiches, with cold cuts — your imagination is the only limit!*

# LACTO-FERMENTED VEGETABLES

PREPARATION: 30 MIN · REST: 48 H · STORAGE: 3 MONTHS

## INGREDIENTS

*Brine:* 2 ½ tbsp. (37 ml) salt • 6 cups (1.5 l) spring water

*For pink pickles:* ½ red beet • ½ red meat (or watermelon) radish • ½ Chioggia beet • ¼ carrot • 4 large pink radishes • 1 piece black radish

*For yellow/orange pickles:* ½ yellow beet •1 yellow carrot • 1 gold ball turnip

*For green pickles:* ½ fennel bulb (very fresh and unstained) • 3 large kiwifruits (hard, unripe) • 1 large green onion

**1.** Prepare the brine by mixing the salt into the water.

**2.** Wash the vegetables using a brush and running water. Peel the root vegetables and slice them finely using a mandoline slicer. Halve the fennel, and then cut one halve in three. Peel the kiwifruits and cut them into thick slices. Cut the onion in four.

**3.** Wash the jars with very hot, soapy water. Rinse them well (but do not wipe them).

**4.** Arrange the vegetables inside each jar, dividing them by color (or in a gradient, if you prefer). Pour the brine into the jars, leaving ¾ inch (2 cm) between the rim and the vegetables. Wedge a wooden stick washed in very hot water against the last vegetable slice, to keep all the vegetables submerged. If any vegetables float to the surface, they'll rot and the pickles will be ruined.

**5.** Screw the lid on. Leave to rest at room temperature for 36 to 48 hours, until the brine starts to lightly fizz, a sign that the fermentation is well under way. A pleasant, slightly sour smell will waft out.

**6.** Transfer the jars to the fridge. Wait 8 to 10 days before tasting. Until opened, the pickles will keep for months in a cool place (at the bottom of the fridge or in a basement).

*I usually make my homemade pickles with vegetables from my garden or the market: homemade pickles are cheaper, simpler and tastier than store-bought pickles. By stacking them in colored layers, you will create a beautiful product — good enough to eat!*

# PICKLES

FOR 2-CUP (500 ML) JAR · PREPARATION: 25 MIN · STORAGE: 1 YEAR

**INGREDIENTS**

4 or 5 florets purple cauliflower • 6 or 7 round pink radishes • ¼ Chioggia beet • 1 large orange carrot • 1 large yellow carrot • 4 or 5 florets white cauliflower • 4 or 5 florets romanesco • 3 or 4 sprigs thyme • 1 cup (250 ml) rice vinegar • ¼ cup (60 ml) water • 1 tbsp. (15 ml) turbinado (or raw) sugar • 1 tsp. (5 ml) gray salt • 1 tsp. (5 ml) coriander seeds

**1.** Wash all of the vegetables under running water.

**2.** Combine the vinegar, water, sugar and salt in a pot or bowl.

**3.** Halve the cauliflower and broccoli florets, as well as the radishes, if they are large.

**4.** Peel the carrots and slice or dice them.

**5.** Wash a large jar with very hot, soapy water. Arrange the vegetables tightly against each other, following the color gradient of the rainbow. Add the coriander seeds and sprigs of thyme.

**6.** Pour in the brine and seal the jar. Let rest for at least 2 weeks before tasting. Refrigerate once opened.

**Good to know:** if you don't want to use rice vinegar, you can use white wine vinegar instead, which may be cheaper and is equally mild. Avoid white vinegar, which is too strong and acidic, or boil it with water (60% vinegar, 40% water) and a little sugar to cut the acidity.

# MAIN COURSES

## AND
## SIDE DISHES

*One concept, two recipes! The first dish is crudités on a bun, slathered with a generous layer of garlic and herb flavored soft soy cheese. Contrary to what you might think, this light "hamburger" tastes great thanks to the moistness of the vegetables and the creaminess of the cheese. For the second recipe, I thought of creating tea sandwiches with goat cheese, setting the tone for Ms. Carrot, Ms. Beet and Mr. Spinach — delicious!*

# CRUDITÉS SANDWICHES

## • CRUDITÉS ON A BUN

FOR 4 PEOPLE · PREPARATION: 25 MIN · COOKING: 1 MIN · STORAGE: 2 DAYS

**INGREDIENTS**

½ small head red cabbage (about 1 cup [250 ml] shredded) • 1 small handful purple radish sprouts • 1 ½ small Chioggia beets • 1 nice tomato • 1 large orange carrot • 1 yellow beet (or 1 yellow carrot) • 8 leaves butterhead lettuce • 1 handful alfalfa or leek sprouts • 4 large burger buns • ¾ cup (175 ml) garlic and herb soft soy cheese

**1.** Wash all vegetables.

**2.** Peel the root vegetables. Slice them and the cabbage very finely with a mandoline slicer.

**3.** Finely slice the tomato.

**4.** Wash the lettuce leaves, and remove and discard the ribs.

**5.** Slice the burger buns in half (if not already sliced). Toast them for 1 minute. Spread cheese on each side.

**6.** On the bottom bun, arrange the red cabbage, radish sprouts, Chioggia beet, tomato, orange carrot, yellow beet, alfalfa and leek sprouts and, finally, the lettuce. Cover with the top bun, and insert a toothpick to hold the vegetables in place. Eat immediately or wrap in plastic wrap.

# CRUDITÉS SANDWICHES CONTINUED

### • TEA SANDWICH SURPRISE

FOR 4 PEOPLE · PREPARATION: 25 MIN · REST: 30 MIN · STORAGE: 2 DAYS

## INGREDIENTS

*Spinach spread:* 2 ½ tbsp. (37 ml) cooked spinach leaves (about ⅔ cup [150 ml] raw) • ½ cup (125 ml) goat cheese • salt

*Carrot spread:* 1 small carrot, cooked • ⅓ cup (75 ml) goat cheese • 1 pinch curry powder • salt

*Beet spread:* ½ small beet, cooked • ⅓ cup (75 ml) goat cheese • salt and black pepper

• 8 large slices sandwich bread

1. Blend the ingredients for each spread. Place each in a separate bowl.

2. Spread the spinach spread onto a slice of bread. Place another slice of bread on top. Spread the carrot spread onto that slice of bread, add another slice of bread on top, and spread the beet spread on it. Finish with another slice of bread. Follow this same procedure with the rest of the spreads and slices of bread (you will have made two large sandwiches).

3. Wrap each sandwich in plastic wrap and chill for 30 minutes. Cut the crusts off. Slice each sandwich three times on the diagonal, creating eight small sandwiches from each large sandwich. Secure each tea sandwich with a toothpick and serve.

*I am proud to be able to cook (and show you) the carrots from my own garden! I grow various colored varieties because of the difference in taste from one carrot to the next and to create beautiful dishes. The vitamin and antioxidant content is a huge benefit, which can vary depending on the variety. Cosmic Purple carrots (with their purple flesh and orange heart) and Spanish Black carrots (with their purple flesh and light yellow heart) are naturally rich in beta-carotenes (orange) but also in anthocyanins (purple). Atomic Red carrots, which are bright red, are rich in lycopene, like tomatoes! Jaune du Doubs carrots contain lutein, and Blanche de Küttingen carrots have no pigment!*

# BALSAMIC ROASTED HERITAGE CARROTS WITH YOGURT AND POMEGRANATE SAUCE

FOR 4 PEOPLE · PREPARATION: 30 MIN · COOKING: 50 MIN · STORAGE: 3 DAYS

### INGREDIENTS

12 heritage carrots (white, yellow, orange, red and purple) · ½ cube vegetable bouillon · 3 tbsp. (45 ml) olive oil · oregano · 3 tbsp. (45 ml) balsamic vinegar · 1 tbsp. (15 ml) honey · 1 cup (250 ml) sheep's milk yogurt · 1 small pomegranate · salt and black pepper

**1.** Preheat oven to 350°F (180°C). Wash the carrots by brushing them under running water. Do not peel them. You can leave about 1 inch (2–3 cm) of the carrot tops, if you like. Arrange the carrots from darkest to lightest on a sheet pan.

**2.** Sprinkle a crushed bouillon cube on top, add 2 cups (500 ml) of water and mix well. Cover with aluminum foil and roast for 30 minutes. Turn the carrots over halfway through the cooking time.

**3.** Remove the foil and add the olive oil, balsamic vinegar and honey. Sprinkle with oregano, mix and continue cooking uncovered for 20 to 30 minutes, basting the carrots regularly. Add a bit of water if the mixture looks too dry.

**4.** While the carrots cook, whisk the yogurt with a pinch of salt and pepper.

**5.** Remove the seeds from the pomegranate.*

**6.** Once the carrots are nicely roasted, salt and pepper them and serve with the yogurt and pomegranate seeds.

**\*Tip:** to easily remove the seeds from the pomegranate, cut the fruit into quarters and plunge them into a bowl of cold water. Expel the seeds while keeping the fruit underwater to prevent juice from splashing and staining. Discard the peel and white membrane. Strain the seeds.

*A dish such as this makes filling up on vitamins a delight! Simple vegetables — nicely chopped, harmoniously proportioned and beautifully presented — are drizzled with olive oil and sprinkled with salt and pepper — and you're done! To show you that we still have plenty of choice during the winter, I've created two versions. It's up to you to choose either one or blend the two.*

# ROASTED WINTER VEGETABLES

FOR 2–4 PEOPLE · PREPARATION: 30 MIN · COOKING: 30 MIN · STORAGE: 3 DAYS

**INGREDIENTS**

*Version 1:* 4 cloves garlic • 1 ½ oz. (40 g) Chinese artichokes • 1 head bok choy • 4 Brussels sprouts • 1 large yellow carrot • 4 oz. (120 g) red kuri squash • ¼ Chioggia beet • 1 purple radish

*Version 2:* 2 large red onions • 7 pink radishes • 1 large orange carrot • ½ yellow beet • 1 leek • broccoli florets • 1 parsnip

• Olive oil • dried thyme • salt • pepper

## • VERSION 1

**1.** Peel the garlic cloves, chop them in half and remove the green germ.

**2.** Rinse the Chinese artichokes and rub them in a dish towel. Rinse the bok choy, slice it and chop the slices in half.

**3.** Wash the Brussels sprouts. Peel the carrot and the Chioggia beet. Slice or dice them. Wash the red kuri squash and purple radish. Dice them (same size as the carrots).

## • VERSION 2

**1.** Peel and chop the red onion in four, and then halve each quarter. Chop off and discard any leaves from the radishes. Carefully wash the radish bulbs.

**2.** Peel the carrot, yellow beet and parsnip. Slice or dice them.

**3.** Cut the leek into sections and rinse well. Chop the broccoli florets into smaller pieces and rinse well.

## • FOR BOTH VERSIONS

**4.** Preheat oven to 350°F (180°C). Arrange the vegetables on a sheet pan, following the color gradient of a rainbow.

**5.** Drizzle with olive oil, and sprinkle with thyme, salt and pepper. Add a bit of water.

**6.** Cover with aluminum foil and roast for 20 minutes. Remove the foil and roast for an additional 10 minutes.

*Hasselback potatoes, a Swedish recipe, are increasingly popular. The potatoes are thinly sliced about halfway through, with the bottoms remaining intact. The easiest way to accomplish this is to put the whole unpeeled potato between two chopsticks, which prevent the blade from chopping through the whole vegetable. When the potatoes are cooked, the slices open, creating an accordion effect that is as beautiful as it is delicious! In this colored version, the orange flesh of the sweet potato rubs shoulders with blue potatoes and red- and yellow-skinned potatoes. To play up the complementary rainbow colors, add a few ears of corn and tomatoes from the garden.*

# HASSELBACK POTATOES WITH ROASTED CORN AND TOMATOES

FOR 6 PEOPLE · PREPARATION: 30 MIN · COOKING: 1 ½ H · STORAGE: 3 DAYS

### INGREDIENTS

1 large sweet potato · 2 red-skinned potatoes · 2 blue potatoes · 2 yellow-skinned potatoes · 2 very ripe tomatoes · 2 ears corn · olive oil · 6 cloves garlic · 1 tbsp. (15 ml) oregano · salt · freshly ground black pepper

**1.** Preheat oven to 375°F (190°C). Brush the sweet potato and potatoes under running water.

**2.** Using a very sharp knife, slice the potatoes along the width every ⅛ inch (3 mm). To keep the knife from slicing through the whole potato, place two chopsticks along each side, so the knife stops at the right place (the thickness of the chopsticks).

**3.** Wash the potatoes to remove the starch, which would keep the slices stuck together as they cook. Slice the tomatoes.

**4.** Arrange the vegetables by color in a large casserole dish (leave space for the corn, which you will add later. Add the garlic (without peeling it). Drizzle with olive oil,

and sprinkle with oregano, salt and pepper. Add a little water to the bottom of the dish. Cover with a lid or aluminum foil.

**5.** Bake for 40 minutes, basting from time to time (three times).

**6.** Uncover, add the corn and baste it with a little cooking juice, and continue baking for 20 minutes, until the potatoes are lightly browned.

**Note:** since sweet potatoes cook more quickly than potatoes, you can choose one that is larger than the potatoes.

*Purists will tell you that there is only one way to make a good ratatouille: cooking the tomatoes, peppers, zucchini and eggplant separately. The snag is you need four pans (or two, in which case you can only cook two vegetables at a time) and a close eye. I suggest a very easy and pretty variation with a color gradient, which is practical thanks to baking. The result is a mix of deliciously roasted, even caramelized, vegetables.*

# BEAUTIFUL BAKED RATATOUILLE

FOR 4–6 PEOPLE · PREPARATION: 45 MIN · COOKING: 1 1/2 H · STORAGE: 3 DAYS

### INGREDIENTS

3 red onions • 3 red oxheart tomatoes • 1 small red pepper • 3 orange oxheart tomatoes • 1 small orange pepper • 1 yellow zucchini • 1 yellow pepper • 2 eggplants • 2 small green zucchini • 1 green pepper • 8 cloves garlic • 2 tbsp. (30 ml) herbes de Provence (or oregano) • 1 drizzle olive oil • 2 pinches salt • freshly ground pepper • 2 tbsp. (30 ml) cane sugar • ¼ cup (60 ml) tomato paste diluted with ⅓ cup (75 ml) water

**1.** Preheat oven to 400°F (200°C). Wash all vegetables and dice them proportionally.

**2.** Arrange them in a large casserole dish, forming a gradient of rainbow colors.

**3.** Peel the garlic cloves and mince. Spread over the vegetables. Sprinkle with herbes de Provence, drizzle with olive oil and salt and pepper to taste. Bake for 20 minutes, and then lower the temperature to 320°F (160°C).

**4.** After 40 minutes the vegetables will be cooked but not yet caramelized. Coat in the sugar and tomato paste. Continue baking at 320°F (160°C) for 30 minutes.

**5.** Bring the dish to the table, and let your guests marvel at the beautiful presentation before stirring to combine. Serve with rice or sautéed potatoes.

*If you're making a complete meal, why not mix the ingredients up — with a playful and nutritious goal in mind? Add some color! In the winter, we naturally fill up on vitamins with anthocyanins (red cabbage/beets), beta-carotene (carrots, squashes) and chlorophyll (mâche, broccoli), which help boost our chilled bodies.*

# WINTER VEGGIE BOWL WITH LENTILS

**FOR 2 PEOPLE · PREPARATION: 40 MIN · COOKING: 35 MIN · STORAGE: 1 DAY**

**INGREDIENTS**

¾ cup (175 ml) green du Berry lentils • ⅛ red cabbage • 3 oz. (80 g) red kuri squash
• 1 cup (250 ml) broccoli florets • 4 pink radishes • ½ Chioggia beet • 1 small yellow carrot
• 2 handfuls mâche (or corn salad) • 1 handful alfalfa and lentil sprouts • 2 fresh eggs
• salt and freshly ground pepper

**1.** Cook the lentils in a large pot of boiling water for 20 minutes. Taste one toward the end of the cooking time; it should still be firm. Drain the lentils, and then season with a pinch of salt and freshly ground pepper. Leave to cool.

**2.** Finely slice the red cabbage. Place it in a large bowl, salt and mix well by hand.

**3.** Dice the red kuri squash. Rinse it well. Steam along with the broccoli for 12 minutes.

**4.** Finally slice the pink radishes and Chioggia beet using a mandoline slicer. Peel and grate the yellow carrot.

**5.** Carefully wash and dry the mâche.

**6.** To poach the eggs, bring a small saucepan of water to a boil. Once the water is boiling, lower the heat to simmer. Break the eggs into the water. Cook for 3 minutes. Once cooked, carefully remove each egg with a slotted spoon and dry on a dish towel.

**7.** Assemble the veggie bowls by arranging the vegetables in large, deep plates following the colors of the rainbow. Start with the lentils, and then add the mâche, broccoli, sprouts, yellow carrot, red kuri squash, pink radishes, Chioggia beet and red cabbage and, finally, place the poached egg in the middle.

**8.** Chill and serve with a nice, mustardy vinaigrette.

**Good to know:** poach the eggs one at a time if you're having difficulty managing two.

*Want to wow your guests at a summery dinner party? Make this delicious 100% tomato tart, rich in lycopene, the highlight of this vegetable-fruit! If you can find firmer and less juicy varieties, such as San Marzano or Orange Banana, which are generally cultivated to be dried, they will do perfectly. The tomatoes release their juices as they cook, so they can soak the puff pastry. To prevent this from happening, they are salted and left to drain.*

# HERITAGE TOMATO AND PARMESAN TART

FOR 4 PEOPLE · PREPARATION: 30 MIN · REST: 1 H · COOKING: 50 MIN · STORAGE: 3 DAYS

**INGREDIENTS**

2 yellow tomatoes • 2 orange tomatoes • 2 red tomatoes
• 2 black or blue tomatoes (cherry, grape, round or oxheart type, as you prefer) •1 sheet puff pastry
• ⅓ cup (75 ml) tomato paste • 2 tbsp. (30 ml) olive oil • ⅓ cup (75 ml) grated Parmesan cheese • oregano • salt

**1.** Wash the tomatoes. Slice any large ones, and prick the smaller ones with the tip of a knife, leaving them whole. Place the tomatoes in a large colander, salt them lightly and leave them to drain for 1 hour.

**2.** Preheat oven to 350°F (180°C). Roll out the puff pastry on a floured surface. Place the pastry in a tart pan lined with parchment paper.

**3.** Dry the tomatoes in a dish towel. Spread the tomato paste on the bottom of the tart shell. Place the tomatoes inside by color, overlapping them slightly, so the tart is nicely filled.

**4.** Drizzle with olive oil. Sprinkle with parmesan, oregano and salt.

**5.** Bake for 45 to 50 minutes. Enjoy a nice slice of this tart with a green salad dressed with a balsamic vinaigrette.

**Gourmet tip:** you can make a more distinct rainbow by adding white tomatoes, such as White Oxheart or White Pearl, and green varieties, such as Green Zebra and Evergreen (but avoid the traditional, unripe, green tomatoes).

*How do you brighten up a barbecue? To get a complete meal from a single skewer, the vegetables (red onion, red and orange peppers, mushroom, zucchini) are paired with starches (potatoes and corn) and smoked tofu. A drizzle of olive oil and a little thyme and salt, and you're done!*

# VEGGIE AND SMOKED TOFU SKEWERS

FOR 4 PEOPLE · PREPARATION: 30 MIN · COOKING: 10 MIN · STORAGE: 3 DAYS

### INGREDIENTS

8 small potatoes • 8 button mushrooms • 2 tbsp. (30 ml) soy sauce • 3 tbsp. (45 ml) balsamic vinegar • 6 tbsp. (90 ml) olive oil • 2 large red onions • 2 red peppers • 2 orange peppers • 1 block smoked tofu • 2 ears corn • 2 green zucchini • olive oil • thyme • salt

**1.** Wash the potatoes. Boil them for 10 minutes. Check the doneness with the tip of a knife.

**2.** Remove the woody stems from the mushrooms. Wipe them with a damp cloth. Place the mushrooms in a shallow bowl. Mix the soy sauce, balsamic vinegar and olive oil. Pour the mixture over the mushrooms, and leave to marinate while you prepare the rest of the ingredients.

**3.** Peel the onions. Chop them in four.

**4.** Wash the peppers, chop them in four and remove the green stem, white membrane and seeds. Dice the flesh into large chunks.

**5.** Cut the smoked tofu into eight cubes.

**6.** Cut each ear of corn in four.

**7.** Wash the zucchini and slice them.

**8.** Assemble the vegetables on metal skewers (which are sturdier than wooden ones), following a color gradient. Drizzle with a bit of olive oil, and sprinkle with dried thyme and salt.

**9.** Barbecue the skewers or broil them in the oven at 430°F (220°C) for 15 to 20 minutes, turning halfway through.

**10.** Arrange the skewers on a large tray and drizzle with the leftover mushroom marinade. Serve immediately.

*I had the idea for this recipe while buying a mix for minestrone soup in an organic store. Unlike the recipe on the package, which indicated to cook all of the legumes to make a soup, I have opted to make a mixed salad and to cook the beans one after the other in the same pot: 45 minutes for the red kidney beans, 40 minutes for the white kidney beans, 20 minutes for the lentils and 10 minutes for the peas. The carrots, corn and tomatoes make for a highly nutritious and harmoniously colorful dish.*

# HARLEQUIN BEAN SALAD

FOR 6 PEOPLE · PREPARATION: 8 H OF SOAKING + 25 MIN · COOKING: 45 MIN · STORAGE: 3 DAYS

**INGREDIENTS**

¼ cup (60 ml) dry red kidney beans • ¼ cup (60 ml) dry white kidney beans
• ¼ cup (60 ml) green du Berry lentils • ¼ cup (60 ml) black beluga lentils • ½ cup (125 ml) fresh (or frozen) peas
• 1 carrot • ½ cup (125 ml) corn kernels • 6 cherry tomatoes • 2 tbsp. (30 ml) cider vinegar
• ⅓ cup (75 ml) canola oil • 1 tbsp. (15 ml) mustard • salt and freshly ground pepper

**1.** The night before, begin soaking the red and white kidney beans in cold water.

**2.** The day of, bring a large pot of water to a boil. Add the red kidney beans and boil for 5 minutes. Add the white kidney beans and boil for 20 minutes more. Add the lentils and boil for a further 10 minutes.

**3.** Meanwhile, wash the peas. Peel and dice the carrots. Add both vegetables to the pot and boil for 10 minutes.

**4.** Taste the legumes to ensure they are cooked. Continue cooking for a few minutes longer if necessary, but be careful, as the lentils should stay firm. Strain and leave the legumes in a bowl to cool.

**5.** Wash and dice the tomatoes. Add them to the legumes, along with the corn, vinegar, oil and mustard. Salt and pepper to taste. Mix well, adjusting the seasoning as desired.

**Note:** do not salt the water when boiling legumes, as it slows down the cooking time considerably.

*Another rainbow food must. These lovely makis, colored naturally with vegetable juices, take a bit of effort, but you'll be amply rewarded when you slice them and discover geometric forms reminiscent of baroque stained glass. Just beautiful!*

# MAKI

**FOR 4 PEOPLE · PREPARATION: 1 1/2 H · REST: 1 H · COOKING: 20 MIN · STORAGE: 2 DAYS**

**INGREDIENTS**

*Filling:* ½ cucumber, cut lengthwise • ¼ red pepper • ¼ yellow pepper • 1 purple sweet potato • salt

*Colored rice:* 2 cups (500 ml) glutinous (or sticky) rice (about ⅓ cup (75 ml) per color)
• 2 cups (500 ml) spring or filtered water • 3 tbsp. (45 ml) + 2 tsp. (10 ml) rice vinegar
• 1 tbsp. (15 ml) + 1 tsp. (5 ml) sugar • 1 tsp. (5 ml) salt • 2 tbsp. (30 ml) fresh spinach juice
• 1 tsp. (5 ml) turmeric • 3 tbsp. (45 ml) beet juice • ¼ small red cabbage
• 4 nori (seaweed) sheets that are 8 inches (20 cm) long

## • FILLING

**1.** Peel and deseed the cucumber. Chop it into 4 pieces with a diameter of about ¼-inch (6 mm). Salt the pieces and leave to drain in a colander while you prepare the rest of the ingredients.

**2.** To obtain a quarter of each pepper, wash them, cut each in 4, and remove and discard the stems, white membranes and seeds. Cut each quarter lengthwise, to obtain 8 pieces that are about ½ inch (12 mm) long with a diameter of about ¼ inch (6 mm) (or more pieces that, when lined up one after another, make a 7-inch [18 cm] long chain). Salt the pieces of pepper and add them to the colander with the cucumber.

**3.** Peel the sweet potato. Slice off two ½-inch (1 cm) thick slices and boil or steam the slices for 10 minutes. Cut the cooked slices to obtain 4 pieces that are 7 to 8 inches (18–20 cm) long (or 8 pieces that are 3 ½ to 4 inches [9–10 cm] long).

**4.** Wash and finely slice the red cabbage. Place the cabbage slices in a pot and cover with water. Cook covered over low heat for 10 minutes. Drain the cabbage over a bowl to save the purple liquid.

## • RICE

**5.** Rinse the rice well, until the water is no longer cloudy. Leave it to rest in a pot of spring (or filtered) water for 10 minutes.

**6.** Drain the rice. Measure it, and put two-thirds in a large pot with 1 ⅓ cups (325 ml) of water and one-third in a small pot with ⅔ cup (150 ml) purple cabbage water. Cook covered over very, very low heat for 10 minutes. If the rice starts to stick to the bottom of the pot, add a little more water. Let the cooked rice rest, covered, for 10 minutes.

# MAKI CONTINUED

**7.** Add 3 tbsp. (45 ml) of white vinegar, 1 tbsp. (15 ml) of sugar and the salt to the white rice and mix well. Add 1 tsp. (5 ml) of sugar and a pinch of salt to the purple rice. Divide this rice in two. Add the remaining 2 tsp. (10 ml) of vinegar to one of the batches of purple rice, which will turn it blue. Divide the white rice into 4 batches. Add the turmeric to the first batch of white rice, which will turn it yellow; add 2 tbsp. (30 ml) of beet juice to the second batch of white rice, which will turn it pink; add 1 tbsp. (15 ml) of beet juice and a pinch of turmeric to the third batch of white rice, to turn it orange; add the spinach juice to the fourth batch of white rice, to turn it green.

## • SHAPING THE MAKIS

**8.** Place a sheet of nori on a small bamboo mat (or dish towel). Arrange the colored rices in order, using the photo below as a reference. The lines of rice should be about ¼ inch (6 mm) thick and ¾ inch (2 cm) wide. Leave a 1-inch (3 cm) space at the edge of the sheet of nori, so you can seal the roll. Add a piece of cucumber, yellow pepper, red pepper and sweet potato down the center of the nori, on top of the rice. Moisten the clean edge of the sheet of nori with a bit of water. Roll the combination tightly, and seal the edge. Follow the same procedure with the remaining ingredients.

**9.** Chill the rolls for at least 1 hour. Slice them into 1-inch (3 cm) slices. Serve with soy sauce.

*This is definitely the simplest recipe in this book! But it hits its mark, especially with children, who will be dazzled with these green, yellow, orange and pink noodles. It's also a good way to get children to eat whole grains and vegetables.*

# COLORED TAGLIATELLE

**FOR 4 PEOPLE · PREPARATION: 10 MIN · COOKING: 10 MIN · STORAGE: 3 DAYS**

### INGREDIENTS

14 oz. (400 g) whole wheat tagliatelle · 2 tbsp. (30 ml) beet juice · 1 tbsp. (15 ml) tomato paste · 1 tsp. (5 ml) turmeric · 2 tbsp. (30 ml) spinach juice · olive oil · salt

**1.** Bring a large pot of water to a boil.

**2.** Add the tagliatelle and cook according to the package's instructions.

**3.** Put the beet juice, tomato paste, turmeric and spinach juice each in a separate bowl.

**4.** Once the pasta is cooked, drain it. Divide it into four batches, and put each in one of the bowls. Add a drizzle of olive oil and pinch of salt to each bowl, and mix well. Cover and leave to rest for 1 minute before serving.

**Good to know:** the colors intensify after resting. You can make this dish in advance and then reheat it. You can also make other colors of pasta by using blueberry juice (purple) or spirulina (blue; 1 tsp [5 ml] diluted in 2 tbsp. [30 ml] water).

*I know you're hesitant, as this recipe requires time and space, but think of how proud you will be to present these farfalle colored in the shades of the peace flag to your guests! No chemical dyes are used in this pasta, only fruit and vegetable juices and purees, known for their intense pigments. You'll marvel at how flavorful they are. To get it right, use a pasta maker, which will allow you to work like a pro.*

# PEACE FLAG FARFALLE

FOR 4 PEOPLE · PREPARATION: 2 1/2 H · REST: 1 H · COOKING: 3 MIN · STORAGE: 2 DAYS

.................................................................................................................................................

**INGREDIENTS**

*Purple dough:* ¼ cup (60 ml) durum wheat semolina · ¼ cup (60 ml) all-purpose flour · ½ egg white, beaten · 1 tbsp. (15 ml) blueberry juice · 1 tsp. (5 ml) olive oil · 1 pinch salt

*Pink dough:* ¼ cup (60 ml) durum wheat semolina · ¼ cup (60 ml) all-purpose flour · ½ egg white, beaten · 1 tbsp. (15 ml) beet juice · 1 tsp. (5 ml) olive oil · 1 pinch salt

*Orange dough:* ¼ cup (60 ml) durum wheat semolina · ¼ cup (60 ml) all-purpose flour · ½ egg white, beaten · 1 tbsp. (15 ml) tomato paste · 1 tsp. (5 ml) olive oil · 1 pinch salt

*Yellow dough:* ¼ cup (60 ml) durum wheat semolina · ¼ cup (60 ml) all-purpose flour · 1 egg yolk · 2 tsp. (10 ml) water · 1 tsp. (5 ml) olive oil · 1 pinch salt

*Green dough:* ¼ cup (60 ml) durum wheat semolina · ¼ cup (60 ml) all-purpose flour · ½ egg white, beaten · 2 tbsp. (30 ml) spinach leaves · 1 tsp. (5 ml) olive oil · 1 pinch salt

· All-purpose flour · 1 beaten egg white, to form the farfalle

## · COLORED PASTA

**1.** Make each pasta color separately. Mix the semolina, flour and salt in a bowl. Make a well in the center, and add the egg whites (or yolk, depending on the recipe) and the rest of the wet ingredients. Mix the ingredients for a few seconds, until well combined, and then transfer the dough to a work surface.

**2.** Knead it for a few minutes, until it becomes supple and elastic. If it becomes too dry, wet your hands with warm water and work it again. Wrap the dough in a dish towel and let rest for 1 hour at room temperature.

# PEACE FLAG FARFALLE CONTINUED

### • MAKING COLORED TAGLIATELLE WITH A PASTA MAKER

**3.** Using a rolling pin, roll out the purple dough on a floured surface. If it's too dry, it will crumble when run through the machine. Add a little water to make it more supple, if needed. If the dough seems sticky, add a bit more flour. Start with the pasta maker in position 1 (the thickest setting). Place the first batch of dough between the two rollers, turning the handle to start the machine. The dough will become thinner as it passes between the rollers. When the dough comes out of the machine, fold it in two and pass it through the machine again.
Folding the dough helps make it more consistent and hold up better when cooked. Fold the dough a second time and run it through the machine again.

**4.** Put the tagliatelle cutter in the machine. Place the purple sheet of dough into the machine. Turn the handle with one hand and catch the tagliatelle with the other. Arrange them on a flat surface, keeping them separate to prevent them from sticking together. Cover with a dish towel.

**5.** Follow the same procedure with the rest of the colored doughs.

**Good to know:** this fresh pasta freezes very well.

### • FORMING THE FARFALLE

**6.** Take a strip of each color of tagliatelle. Flour the work surface and lay the green tagliatelle flat on it. Brush a little egg white from left to right. Place the yellow tagliatelle above the green one, directly against it, and so on with the rest of the colors. You will get a long rainbow band of pasta. Cut it in two, and place one half above the other, to form a shorter strip with two sets of rainbow colors (see photo on page 78). Flour it.

**7.** Run the strip through the pasta maker to stick the tagliatelle uniformly together and make a long, perfectly flat rainbow strip.

**8.** Using a pasta crimper, cut the strip into 1 ½-inch (4 cm) squares. Brush a little egg white onto a square, fold it in two (with the crimped edges at the left and right) and, using a pair of tweezers, pinch the center to shape the square into farfalle. Proceed accordingly with the rest of the squares. Leave the farfalle to dry on the work surface.

**9.** Repeat this technique with the remaining tagliatelle.

**10.** Bring a large pot of water to a boil, and add a generous pinch of salt and a drizzle of olive oil. Once the water boils, add the pasta and cook for 3 minutes. Strain the farfalle and return it to the pot. Eat immediately with olive oil.

*This recipe is another rainbow food must! Wow your guests with the color gradient made by red cabbage, peppers and broccoli. The sweet flavor of the peppers and the softness of the pizza dough contrast with the stronger character of the cabbage, mustard and feta cheese.*

# RAINBOW PIZZA

FOR 4 PEOPLE · PREPARATION: 45 MIN · COOKING: 50 MIN · STORAGE: 3 DAYS

### INGREDIENTS

1 batch pizza dough · 1 large piece red cabbage · 1 red pepper · 1 orange pepper · ½ yellow pepper · 1 small head broccoli · ¼ cup (60 ml) whole-grain mustard · ½ cup (125 ml) feta cheese · thyme · salt

**1.** Finely slice the red cabbage. Put it in a bowl with the salt and mix well. Leave to rest while you prepare the other ingredients. This helps soften the cabbage.

**2.** Preheat oven to 425°F (220°C). Cut the peppers lengthwise into quarters. Remove and discard the stems and seeds. Place the peppers on a sheet pan and bake for 20 to 25 minutes, until the peel is lightly browned. Transfer to a bowl and cover with a plate. Once the peppers have cooled, peel them and cut them into thin strips, around ½ inch (1 cm) wide.

**3.** Boil or steam the broccoli for 7 to 8 minutes.

**4.** Roll out the pizza dough on a floured surface. Place it on a floured pizza pan. Coat with mustard.

**5.** Arrange the broccoli in the middle. Add the yellow peppers around in a circle, and then the orange pepper, followed by the red pepper and the red cabbage. Sprinkle the feta cheese and thyme on top.

**6.** Bake for 20 minutes. Serve immediately with a green salad.

*Rainbow food isn't confined to a color gradient: you can also express the rainbow on your plates in festive culinary paintings! Here, an omelet is adorned with the green of arugula, the red of cherry tomatoes, the yellow-orange of zucchini blossoms and the purple of borage blossoms, which have a lovely cucumber flavor.*

# ARUGULA, ZUCCHINI BLOSSOM AND BORAGE BLOSSOM OMELET

FOR 2 PEOPLE · PREPARATION: 20 MIN · COOKING: 20 MIN · STORAGE: 2 DAYS

### INGREDIENTS

5 eggs • 5 zucchini blossoms • 1 small handful arugula • 8 to 10 cherry tomatoes • a few freshly picked borage blossoms • 1 tbsp. (15 ml) olive oil • 1 tsp. (5 ml) oregano • salt and freshly ground pepper

**1.** Break the eggs and beat them with a fork. Add salt to taste.

**2.** Wash and dry the arugula. Rinse the tomatoes and dice them. Remove the pistils from the zucchini blossoms.

**3.** Heat up a small pan over high heat. Add the olive oil, wait for a few seconds (it must not smoke) and then pour in the beaten eggs. Fold the edges gently with a wooden spatula. Place the zucchini blossoms and cherry tomatoes on the eggs while they are still liquid. Keep folding the edges to let the liquid egg flow under the cooked egg.

**4.** Lower the heat, cover and cook for 2 or 3 minutes, until the top of the omelet is done.

**5.** Sprinkle with pepper and oregano, and garnish with borage blossoms. Serve the omelette with a green salad.

*I am particularly fond of this Italian pasta shaped like buns, especially when they are sautéed after being poached. To make colored variants, you can use colored tubers, such as sweet potatoes, purple potatoes, blue potatoes, or mashed potatoes colored with spinach, beets or turmeric. If the yield looks like more than you'll need, remember that the uncooked gnocchi can be frozen without problem.*

# GNOCCHI

FOR 6 PEOPLE · PREPARATION: 1 1/2 H · COOKING: 20 MIN · STORAGE: 2 DAYS

**INGREDIENTS**

1 large baking potato • 1 tbsp. (15 ml) cooked and blended spinach • 1 small orange sweet potato • ¼ small beet, cooked • 1 small purple sweet potato • 1 small blue potato • 2 tbsp. (30 ml) potato starch (or cornstarch) • 1 ¾ cup (425 ml) all-purpose flour • 1 pinch turmeric • olive oil • salt

**1.** Peel all of the potatoes and cut into a large dice. Steam for 15 minutes.

**2.** Yellow dough: press a third of the cooked baking potato through a mesh strainer (do not use an electric mixer, which will make the dough too elastic). Add ¼ cup (60 ml) of flour, 1 tsp. (5 ml) of potato starch, a pinch of turmeric and salt to taste. Knead until the ingredients are well mixed and a dough is formed. Shape into a ball. It should have the consistency of a pie dough. If it is too soft, add a little flour and knead a bit more, until desired consistency is reached.

**3.** Green dough: follow the same procedure, using a third of the baking potato, the cooked spinach, ¼ to ⅓ cup (60 to 75 ml) of flour and 1 tsp. (5 ml) of potato starch. Don't forget to add salt.

**4.** Pink dough: follow the same procedure, using a third of the baking potato, the cooked beets, ⅓ to ½ cup (75 to 125 ml) of flour and 1 tsp. (5 ml) of potato starch.

**5.** Purple and orange doughs: follow the same procedure with the relevant sweet potatoes, using ¼ cup (60 ml) of flour and 1 tsp. (5 ml) of potato starch for each color.

**6.** Blue dough: follow the same procedure with the blue potato, using ¼ cup (60 ml) of flour and 1 tsp. (5 ml) of potato starch.

**7.** To shape the gnocchi, roll each color of dough on a floured surface, forming a ½-inch (1 cm) wide rope. Cut each rope crosswise about every 1 inch (2–3 cm). Shape each small section into little balls with your hands. Flatten them gently against the floured surface and roll them with a fork to mark them.

**8.** Bring a large pot of water to a boil. Add the gnocchi. They are cooked when they float to the surface. Drain.

**9.** Serve with tomato sauce or sauté in a pan with a touch of olive oil.

# DESSERTS

*To embark on this sweet chapter, here's a recipe that couldn't be simpler: a fruit platter! But pay attention, as this isn't your average fruit platter. It presents an array of beautifully cut fruits in a gradient of rainbow colors. While you may be tempted by the assortment of colors available, try to buy fruits that are in season.*

# FRUIT PLATTERS

FOR 2–4 PEOPLE · PREPARATION: 40 MIN · STORAGE: 1 DAY

......................................................................................................................................

## INGREDIENTS

**Summer platter:** 1 mango "cheek" (½ unpeeled mango cut along the pit) • 6 or 7 strawberries
• 1 cup (250 ml) raspberries • 1 cup (250 ml) red currants • 1 cup (250 ml) blueberries • 2 bananas
• ¼ pineapple • 1 red dragon fruit • 1 lime • 1 dash lemon juice

**Winter platter:** ½ mango • ½ red pomegranate • 1 persimmon • 1 lemon • 2 passion fruits • 1 apple
• 1 clementine • 1 small pear • 2 kiwifruits • 1 banana • poppy seeds

## • SUMMER PLATTER

**1.** Using a sharp knife, cut a checkerboard pattern into the flesh of the mango, without peeling it. Turn it inside out, like a sock, to reveal the chunks.

**2.** Peel only one section of the bananas. With the tip of a knife, slice the banana flesh, stopping at the peel. Drizzle with lemon juice.

**3.** Using a sharp knife, slice the lime in a zigzag pattern along its width.

**4.** Slice the pineapple, and then run a knife along the bottom, along the skin, to peel it.

**5.** Wash the strawberries and halve some of them. Rinse the raspberries and currants. Halve the dragon fruit.

**6.** Take a large serving plate. First place the large fruits (mango, dragon fruit), then the medium-sized fruits (bananas, pineapple, lime) and then randomly fill in with the small fruits. Chill before serving.

# FRUIT PLATTERS CONTINUED

### • WINTER PLATTER

**1.** Using a sharp knife, cut a checkerboard pattern into the flesh of the mango, without peeling it. Turn it inside out, like a sock, to reveal the chunks.

**2.** Peel only one section of the banana. With the tip of a knife, slice the banana flesh, stopping at the peel. Drizzle with lemon juice.

**3.** Cut the kiwifruits in a zigzag pattern along their width, and then open them.

**4.** Wash the persimmon, passion fruit and lemon, and half each along its width. Peel the clementine.

**5.** Halve the pomegranate. Plunge both halves in a bowl of cold water. Expel a few seeds, keeping the fruit underwater, so the juices don't stain; leave a few sections whole. Throw away any bits of peel and white membrane. Drain the seeds and fruit on a cloth.

**6.** Take a large serving platter. Arrange the fruits as shown in the photo opposite.

*Here's a way to encourage children to cook like gourmets and learn about colors —
and a fun way to get them to eat fruits. I'm partial to late-summer fruits, but feel free
to change things up and use whatever is in season.*

# FRUIT SKEWERS

FOR 6 PEOPLE · PREPARATION: 40 MIN · STORAGE: 2 DAYS

**INGREDIENTS**

12 large blackberries · 2 figs · 12 strawberries · 12 large raspberries · ½ melon · ¼ pineapple · 2 kiwifruits

*Chocolate sauce (optional):* 7 squares (7 oz. / 200 g) dark chocolate (or milk chocolate, for children)
· ⅓ cup (75 ml) coconut oil

**1.** Rinse the blackberries, raspberries and
strawberries under running water.

**2.** Halve the figs, and then cut the halves
into three. Dice the melon and pineapple.

**3.** Peel the kiwifruits, halve them and then
dice the halves.

**4.** Put the fruit onto the skewers following
the color gradient.

**5.** Chill the assembled skewers. Melt the
chocolate in a double boiler. Serve the
chocolate sauce with the fruit skewers.

*Great at breakfast, as a snack or after a good workout, these chia seed puddings come in technicolor shades, with kiwifruit, pineapple, orange, raspberries and blueberries. For a multi-fruit version in the same glass, simply stack the different layers from green to purple.*

# CHIA PUDDING

FOR 5 PEOPLE · PREPARATION: 1 1/4 H · REST: 1 1/2 H · STORAGE: 1 TO 2 DAYS

### INGREDIENTS

*White layer:* ½ cup (125 ml) chia seeds • 3 cups (750 ml) almond milk • ⅓ cup (75 ml) sugar

*Green layer:* 1 tbsp. (15 ml) chia seeds • ¼ cup (60 ml) almond milk • 1 small kiwifruit • 1 tbsp. (15 ml) sugar • 1 handful spirulina

*Yellow layer:* 1 tbsp. (15 ml) chia seeds • ¼ cup (60 ml) almond milk • ⅓ cup (75 ml) cubed pineapple blended with 2 tsp. (10 ml) sugar and 1 pinch turmeric

*Orange layer:* 1 tbsp. (15 ml) chia seeds • ¼ cup (60 ml) almond milk • ½ orange blended with 2 tsp. (10 ml) sugar and 1 tsp. (5 ml) raspberry (or beet) juice

*Pink layer:* 1 tbsp. (15 ml) chia seeds • ¼ cup (60 ml) almond milk • ¼ cup (60 ml) raspberries (fresh or frozen) blended with 2 tsp. (10 ml) sugar

*Purple layer:* 1 tbsp. (15 ml) chia seeds • ¼ cup (60 ml) almond milk • 2 tbsp. (30 ml) wild blueberries (fresh or frozen) blended with 2 tsp. (10 ml) sugar

*Garnish:* ½ kiwifruit • 5–6 pineapple chunks • 5–6 orange wedges • 5–9 raspberries • 1 handful blueberries •1 star fruit • 1 tbsp. (15 ml) poppy seeds

**1.** To make the white layer, put the chia seeds, almond milk and sugar in a bowl. Beat. Wait 2 minutes, and beat again. Let rest for 1 hour at room temperature.

**2.** To make the green layer, put the chia seeds, almond milk, sugar and spirulina in a bowl. Beat. Wait 2 minutes, and beat again. Let rest for 20 minutes at room temperature. While the mixture is resting, peel the kiwifruit and blend it with 2 tsp. (10 ml) of sugar. Add it to the chia seed/almond milk mixture. Let rest 20 minutes more.

**3.** Follow the same procedure with the remaining four fruits.

**4.** While puddings are resting, prepare the fruits for the garnish. Wash the star fruit and slice thinly. Place three slices into every glass, ensuring they stick to the sides of the glasses.

**5.** Scoop a layer of the green kiwifruit pudding into the first glass, and then add a layer of the white pudding. Place a few pieces of kiwifruit and a slice of star fruit on top. Follow the same procedure with the other fruits. Chill for at least 1 hour before serving.

*Here is a fruit bowl that's actually a meal, which can be eaten for breakfast or after returning from a good walk. The layers of chia seeds and oats along with the plethora of winter fruits create a vitamin-packed dish that is sure to give your body a boost.*

# FRUIT BOWL

FOR 2 PEOPLE · PREPARATION: 25 MIN · COOKING: 3 MIN · REST: 1 H · STORAGE: 2 DAYS

### INGREDIENTS

½ cup (125 ml) chia seeds • 1 ⅔ cups (400 ml) almond milk • 3 tbsp. (45 ml) maple syrup • ½ banana • 1 mango "cheek" (see page 91) • 1 mandarin • 1 kiwifruit • ½ persimmon • ½ pomegranate • 2 tbsp. (30 ml) blueberries (frozen) • 1 handful hazelnuts • 1 cup (250 ml) rolled oats • poppy seeds

**1.** Put the chia seeds, almond milk and maple syrup in a bowl. Beat. Wait 2 minutes and beat again. Let rest for 1 hour at room temperature.

**2.** Peel and slice the banana. Finely dice the mango and persimmon. Peel the mandarin and separate it into segments. Peel and slice the kiwifruit. Remove the seeds from the pomegranate.*

**3.** Chop the hazelnuts in half (a chef's knife works best for this), and roast them for a few minutes in a pan to make them crunchy.

**4.** Divide the oats into two large bowls or deep plates. Pour the hydrated chia seeds over top. Arrange the fruits neatly over the chia seed mixture, following the gradient of the colors of the rainbow. Add the hazelnuts and poppy seeds. Enjoy the pudding with a nice cup of tea.

**\*Tip:** to easily remove the seeds from the pomegranate, cut the fruit into quarters and plunge into a bowl of cold water. Expel the seeds while keeping the fruit underwater, to prevent juice from splashing and staining. Discard the peel and white membrane. Strain the seeds.

*This panna cotta is a wonder for both the eyes and the taste buds! Every multicolored spoonful has a palette of flavors that's reminiscent of a milky and fruity soft candy. Don't be too heavy-handed with the agar, as too much will give the dish an overly firm "jelly" consistency.*

# FRUIT PANNA COTTA

**FOR 4 PEOPLE · PREPARATION: 30 MIN · COOKING: 5 MIN · REST: 3 H · STORAGE: 3 DAYS**

## INGREDIENTS

1 tbsp. (15 ml) blueberry puree • 2 tbsp. (30 ml) raspberry puree (strained, to remove seeds) • 2 tbsp. (30 ml) apricot puree • 2 tbsp. (30 ml) mango puree • 2 tbsp. (30 ml) kiwifruit puree with 1 pinch spirulina • 1 ⅔ cups (400 ml) almond milk • 1 ¼ cups (300 ml) liquid almond (or soy) cream • ½ cup (125 ml) turbinado (or raw) sugar • 1 tbsp. (15 ml) cornstarch • 2 tsp. (10 ml) agar

**1.** Put each fruit puree into separate large bowls. Take out 4 flexible molds (or glasses, if desired).

**2.** Pour the almond milk, almond cream, sugar, cornstarch and agar into a saucepan. Whisk the mixture over low heat until it begins to boil. Turn the heat off.

**3.** Pour ½ cup (125 ml) of this mixture into the bowl with the blueberry puree, whisk well and then pour into the molds (around 2 tablespoons [30 ml] of colored cream per mold). Chill in the freezer for 5 minutes. Cover the saucepan so the cream does not congeal too quickly.

**4.** Pour ½ cup (125 ml) of the cream mixture into the bowl with the raspberry puree, and whisk well. Take the molds out of the freezer, and add the raspberry cream.

**5.** Follow the same procedure with the rest of the ingredients, following a rainbow color gradient. Finish with a layer of the plain cream mixture (which is white). If the cream congeals in the saucepan, reheat it over low heat.

**6.** Chill the molds in the fridge for at least 3 hours. Unmold the panna cotta and enjoy with cookies.

*This recipe is one of my breakfast staples. Uncooked buckwheat is hydrated and paired with bananas, yogurt and fresh fruit. A guaranteed pick-me-up to take on the day! If you have friends staying over for the weekend, bring them a tray of these beautiful glasses and let them choose their favorite flavor.*

# YOGURT AND FRESH FRUIT WITH RAW BUCKWHEAT GRANOLA

FOR 5 SMALL GLASSES · PREPARATION: 40 MIN (OVER 2 DAYS) · DRYING: 4–6 H · STORAGE: 2 DAYS

**INGREDIENTS**

*Granola:* 3 cups (750 ml) buckwheat (not toasted) • 3 very ripe bananas • 2 ½ tbsp (37 ml) agave syrup

*Fruit and yogurt:* 2 nectarines • 1 large slice melon • 10 medium strawberries • 1 cup (250 ml) raspberries • 1 cup (250 ml) blueberries • 3 ¾ cups yogurt or cream cheese • ⅓ cup (75 ml) cane sugar (optional)

### • GRANOLA

**1.** The day before, soak the buckwheat for 4 hours. Rinse it well after soaking.

**2.** Blend the bananas with the agave syrup. Add them to the buckwheat and stir to combine.

**3.** Dry this mixture in a dehydrator set to 115°F (45°C) for 4 to 5 hours or in a 120°F (50°C) oven for 5 to 6 hours. The buckwheat grains should be perfectly dry and crusty.

**4.** Once cooled, store in an airtight container.

### • FRUIT AND YOGURT

**1.** Peel the nectarines and remove the pits. Finely dice half a nectarine, and blend the rest. Ball about a third of the melon with a melon baller. Blend the rest. Rinse and hull the strawberries. Chop a few and blend the rest. Rinse the raspberries and blueberries. Save a handful as garnish, and blend the rest.

**2.** Mix the yogurt and sugar together.

**3.** Portion out the yogurt among 5 glasses. Add the fruit purees and then the chopped fruit on top. Add 2 tablespoons (30 ml) of granola and serve. Make some granola available to those who may want more.

**Note:** you will have buckwheat granola leftover, which is normal. It wouldn't be very environmentally-friendly to use a dehydrator or oven just for ½ cup (125 ml) of buckwheat, which will be eaten in one sitting.

*This is the dessert I grew up with! In this rainbow version, the traditional sour cherries from my native Berry (France) are replaced by a myriad of colorful summer fruits. Rhubarb for green, yellow plums for yellow, apricots for orange, plums for red and blueberries for purple. The result is quite a cute and cheerful tart, which melts in your mouth thanks to the almond milk.*

# TUTTI-FRUTTI TART

**FOR 6 PEOPLE · PREPARATION: 20 MIN · COOKING: 45 MIN · STORAGE: 3 DAYS**

**INGREDIENTS**

2 eggs • ½ cup (125 ml) turbinado (or raw) sugar • 1 cup (250 ml) all-purpose or rice flour • 1 ⅓ cups (325 ml) almond milk • 1 stalk green rhubarb • about 15 yellow plums • 4 apricots • 3 medium red plums • ½ cup blueberries • 2 tbsp. (30 ml) margarine

**1.** Preheat oven to 375°F (190°C). Crack the eggs and beat them along with ⅓ cup (75 ml) of sugar. Gradually add the flour and almond milk, alternating between the two ingredients.

**2.** Peel the rhubarb and slice it. Wash the stone fruits. Halve the apricots, but leave the plums whole. Rinse the blueberries.

**3.** Grease a tart pan with ½ tbsp. (7 ml) of margarine. Pour the dough into the pan. Add the fruit, arranging it in a gradient of rainbow colors.

**4.** Bake for 45 minutes. After 30 minutes, dot the tart with the rest of the margarine and sugar.

**Note:** For a tart such as this, the pits are sometimes left in the smaller stone fruits, to keep the pastry from becoming too moist. However, if children will be eating the dessert, it's best to remove the pits. In that case, bake the tart a little longer, but check it carefully to ensure the top doesn't burn.

*I've miniaturized this famous Australian dessert of meringue and whipped cream, so it's easier to serve and eat than the jumbo version! This version also lets you play with colors and aromas! You can also make six rainbow-gradient pavlovas, as shown in the photo on the left, and thus a range of summer flavors. I also give you a choice between two meringue recipes. The first is a French one, which is easier to make but also tends to color as it cooks if the recipe isn't executed perfectly and also tends to rehydrate rather quickly. The second is a Swiss version that is prepared with a double boiler, which is more stable, is often used for lemon meringue pies and has a nice, crunchy texture when cooked (I prefer the latter recipe for pavlovas, as they must be stored in the fridge).*

# MINI PAVLOVAS

FOR 6 PEOPLE · PREPARATION: 1 1/2 H · COOKING: 1 3/4 H · STORAGE: 1 DAY

### INGREDIENTS

*Meringue:* ¾ cup (175 ml) turbinado (or raw) sugar • 3 egg whites, room temperature • 2 or 3 drops lemon juice

*Toppings:* ¾ cup (175 ml) heavy cream (or whipping cream) • 1 ½ tbsp. (22 ml) turbinado (or raw) sugar • ½ banana • zest and juice from 1 lime • 3 thin slices lime • 1 yellow nectarine • 2 ripe apricots • 3 large strawberries • 10 raspberries • 15 blueberries

### • FRENCH MERINGUE

**1.** Blend the sugar so it has the consistency of icing sugar (the meringue will take shape more quickly, the sugar crystals will melt more easily and the meringue will not look granular after being cooked).

**2.** Pour the egg whites into the mixer bowl, along with the lemon juice, and start to beat them slowly to loosen them. Once they start to foam, sprinkle in the sugar. Gradually increase the speed of the mixer until you have a thick, shiny meringue.

### • SWISS MERINGUE

**1.** Blend the sugar, using the same procedure as the French meringue recipe.

**2.** Bring a saucepan of water to a boil. As the water heats up, start to slowly beat the egg whites along with the sugar in a large stainless steel or heatproof glass bowl using a hand mixer. The mixture will start to look frothy and white but will not yet have much volume. Place the bowl over the saucepan of boiling water, creating a double boiler. Gradually increase the speed of the mixer. The meringue will double in volume and become shiny as it cooks. Take it off the heat and continue to beat until it cools.

# MINI PAVLOVAS CONTINUED

**3.** Preheat oven to 220°F (100°C). Scoop the meringue into a piping bag with a round or star tip. Stick a piece of parchment paper to a large sheet pan with four beads of meringue. Form six nests by spiraling the meringue, or create six meringue balls and spread them out to the side, creating a shallow well in the center. Bake for 1 hour. Lower the oven to 175°F (80°C) and continue baking for 45 minutes. The meringues are done when you can easily unstick them from the parchment paper. If they stick, continue baking.

**4.** While the meringues are baking, wash the mixer bowl and beaters, and place them in the freezer for 2 hours. Pour the cream into the mixer bowl for the last 20 minutes of cooling (it should not freeze).

**5.** Wash all of the fruit. Slice the banana and drizzle with lemon juice; peel and dice the nectarine; slice the apricots; dice the strawberries. The raspberries and blueberries simply need to be rinsed.

**6.** Once the meringues are baked and cooled, prepare the whipped cream by putting the sugar in the mixer bowl and whipping at maximum speed for 8 to 10 minutes, until it forms soft peaks. The beaters leave very clear marks.

**7.** Spread the whipped cream over the meringues. Arrange the fruit by color or following a gradient of rainbow colors. Chill for at least 1 hour before serving.

**Gourmet tip:** you can make the meringue the day before and the whipped cream 1 to 3 hours before serving.

*Certain pastries seem almost too complex, with their high-end allure. If you follow the instructions in the recipe for this multi-fruit tart and put your heart into it, you'll get excellent results! Its characteristic feature, besides its vitamin-packed rainbow of fruit, is its vegetarian ganache made with white chocolate, tofu and coconut milk — as light as you could wish. The little extra touch is the glaze that gives the fruit a glossy look.*

# MULTI-FRUIT TART

FOR 6 PEOPLE · PREPARATION: 2 1/4 H · REST: 2 H · COOKING: 45 MIN · STORAGE: 2 DAYS

## INGREDIENTS

*Shortcrust pastry:* 2 ¼ cups (560 ml) all-purpose flour • ⅓ cup (75 ml) turbinado (or raw) sugar • 1 pinch salt • ¼ cup (60 ml) almond butter • 2 ½ tbsp. (37 ml) olive oil • ⅓ cup (75 ml) oat milk

*Vegetarian pastry cream:* 3 medium nectarines, peeled and pits removed • ⅓ cup (75 ml) turbinado (or raw) sugar • ⅓ cup (75 ml) water • 3 tbsp. (45 ml) lemon juice • 1 bar white chocolate (6 oz. [180 g]) • 3 oz. (80 g) firm tofu • ¾ cup (175 ml) coconut cream

*Topping:* 2 kiwifruits • ¼ fresh pineapple • 2 nectarines, peeled and pits removed (or 4 peach halves in syrup) • ¼ melon • 14 medium strawberries • 1 small bunch red grapes • ½ tsp. (2 ml) agar

## • SHORTCRUST PASTRY

**1.** In a large bowl, combine the flour, sugar and salt. Make a well in the center of the dry ingredients, and add the almond butter, olive oil and oat milk. Mix with a fork to combine, and then form a ball by hand, without working the dough too much (to prevent it from becoming too elastic). Let rest for 1 hour in the fridge.

**2.** Preheat oven to 350°F (180°C). Roll out the dough on a floured work surface or between two sheets of parchment paper, if you find that easier.

**3.** Place the dough in a tart pan lined with parchment paper. Shape the edges nicely. Cover the dough with another sheet of parchment paper and follow with pie weights or dry beans. This cooking method is called "blind" baking.

**4.** Bake for 25 minutes (approximately; it will depend on the size of the pan), and then leave to cool on a rack.

# MULTI-FRUIT TART CONTINUED

### • PASTRY CREAM

**5.** Place the mixer bowl, beaters and the coconut cream in the freezer for 1 hour before making the cream.

**6.** Finely dice the nectarines. Place them in a saucepan with the sugar, water and lemon juice. Cover and cook over low heat for 10 minutes, stirring occasionally.

**7.** Strain the mixture and save the juice. Put the juice aside in a small saucepan (you will use it to make the glaze).

**8.** Melt the white chocolate in a double boiler. Blend it with the cooked nectarines and firm tofu, forming a smooth paste.

**9.** Beat the white chocolate mixture with the coconut cream until it is thick and shiny (about 1 minute). You should have a thick, firm ganache.

**10.** Using a soft spatula, fill the cooked tart shell and transfer to the fridge.

### • TOPPING AND GLAZE

**11.** Peel and slice the kiwifruits. Peel the pineapple and cut it into small triangles. Peel and finely slice the nectarines. Remove the rind from the melon and cut the flesh into small triangles. Hull the strawberries and halve any large ones. Wash the grapes and remove the stems.

**12.** Arrange the fruits neatly on the tart shell (you can use the photo as a model). Don't worry overly much about the first layer of fruit, which will sink into the cream, but do pay close attention to the second layer!

**13.** Add the agar to the nectarine juice that was set aside. Bring the mixture to a boil and cook for 30 seconds, whisking regularly. Let the glaze rest at room temperature for 5 minutes, and then coat the fruit on the tart with it.

**14.** Chill for at least 1 hour before serving.

**Good to know:** if you have any leftover fruit, once you've finished covering the tart, blend it to make a multi-fruit smoothie, which will make a great snack or breakfast.

*You'll wow everyone with these sweet and tangy — and colorful — little vegan tarts. A shortcrust pastry that is beautifully crusty, a "raw" almond and vanilla pastry cream, segments of lime, orange, mandarin, pink grapefruit and blood orange, all topped off with a sweet glaze that makes everything shine... Once you try it, you'll be delighted by the mix of citrus flavors. When you try the Moro variety of Sicilian blood oranges, it will be love at first taste!*

# CITRUS TARTLETS

FOR 6 PEOPLE · PREPARATION: 1 3/4 H · REST: 8 H · BAKING : 18 MIN · STORAGE: 2 DAYS

## INGREDIENTS

*"Raw" pastry cream:* ⅓ cup (75 ml) blanched almonds • 2 oz. (70 g) firm tofu • 2 ½ tbsp. (37 ml) agave syrup • 2 tbsp. (30 ml) lemon juice • seeds from 1 vanilla bean

*Shortcrust pastry:* ⅔ cup (150 ml) rice flour • ¾ cup (175 ml) all-purpose flour • ¼ cup (60 ml) turbinado (or raw) sugar • ¼ cup (60 ml) whole almonds, blended • 3 tbsp. (45 ml) coconut oil • ¼ cup (60 ml) almond milk

*Topping:* 3 limes • 3 oranges • 4 mandarins • 2 grapefruits • 4 blood oranges

*Glaze:* ⅓ cup (75 ml) water • 2 ½ tbsp. (37 ml) turbinado (or raw) sugar • 1 tsp. (5 ml) agar

### • PASTRY CREAM

**1.** The day (or 6 hours) before, soak the almonds in a bowl of cold water.

**2.** When they've finished soaking, rinse the almonds. Blend with the tofu, agave syrup, lemon juice and vanilla seeds, until you have a very smooth cream. Transfer to the fridge.

### • SHORTCRUST PASTRY

**3.** Mix the flours with the sugar and almond powder in a bowl. Melt the coconut oil. Pour it and the almond milk into the flour-sugar mixture. Knead the ingredients together and form a ball of dough. Chill for 1 hour.

**4.** Preheat oven to 350°F (180°C). Roll out the dough between two sheets of parchment paper. Divide it into 6 and place each section of dough into a tartlet pan. Bake for 18 minutes. Take the tartlet crusts out of the oven and leave to cool on a rack.

# CITRUS TARTLETS CONTINUED

### • TOPPING

**5.** Cut the citrus fruits into supremes* by first cutting the ends off every fruit. Lay the fruits on one of the flat ends, and remove the peel and pith with a very sharp knife, following the round shape of the fruit. Remove the skin as well, leaving only the fruit. Lay the supremes on a dish towel to dry.

**6.** Fill the tart crusts with the pastry cream. Neatly arrange the citrus supremes, following a rainbow color gradient. Fill any bare areas, where you can see the pastry cream, with the smallest pieces of fruit.

### • GLAZE

**7.** Whisk all ingredients in a small saucepan, bring to a boil and cook for 30 seconds. Coat the tartlets generously using a brush. Chill for at least 1 hour, and then enjoy with a nice cup of Earl Grey tea.

**\*Note:** if you'd like to see the technique to supreme citrus fruits, there are many video tutorials available online.

*Ah, the cheesecake! Some worship it as much as apple pie! However, the recipe won't turn out well if you rush through it. Follow each step carefully, put your heart into it and top it off with fruit purees swirled together using the back of a spoon.*

# FRUIT CHEESECAKE

**FOR 8 PEOPLE · PREPARATION: 2 1/4 H · REST: 6 H + 24 H · COOKING: 45 MIN · STORAGE: 2 DAYS**

## INGREDIENTS

*Filling:* 5 cups (1.25 l) whole sheep's milk yogurt • 1 cup (250 ml) coconut cream • 1 cup (250 ml) turbinado (or raw) sugar • 6 eggs • 1 tbsp. (15 ml) vanilla extract

*Crust:* 14 oz. (400 g) speculas (or other spiced) cookies • ⅔ cup (150 ml) coconut oil

*Colored topping:* 2 tbsp. (30 ml) concentrated raspberry puree (see page 19) • 2 tbsp. (30 ml) concentrated blueberry puree • 2 tbsp. (30 ml) concentrated mango puree • fresh raspberries, blueberries, red currants and mango

**1.** The day before, place the yogurt in a dish towel, knot the top and leave to drain over a large pot for 6 hours in the fridge. The following day, you'll have a thick yogurt. Set aside.

**2.** To prepare the crust, first crumble the cookies and blend them into fine crumbs (or put them in a bag and crush with a rolling pin). There should not be any large pieces.

**3.** Melt the coconut oil, and add it to the cookie crumbs. Mix well.

**4.** Line an 8 ½-inch (22 cm) springform pan with parchment paper (both the bottom and the side). Press the cookie crumb mixture into the pan, using a glass to flatten the mixture along the bottom. Work the cookie crumbs up the side of the pan, pressing with the glass. Preheat oven to 300°F (150°C).

**5.** Make the cheese filling. Gently whip the drained yogurt, coconut cream, sugar, eggs and vanilla, ensuring the mixture stays thick. If you whip it too much, the cheesecake will be too thick once it is baked.

**6.** Pour the cheese filling into the crust. Dot the filling with the concentrated fruit purees, and use the back of a spoon to create swirls and ripples.

**7.** Bake for 45 minutes. Turn off the oven and leave the cheesecake to cool inside. Chill in the fridge for 24 hours.

**8.** Garnish the cheesecake with raspberries, blueberries and a "cheek" of unpeeled mango that you have cut into squares and turned inside out (see page 91).

**Gourmet tip:** keep the yogurt liquid (the whey) to make pancakes or crepes (use half whey, half milk).

*Here's a more digestible version of the traditional tiramisu made with eggs and mascarpone. This recipe calls for aquafaba (the liquid from canned chickpeas, which replaces the egg whites), white chocolate, tofu and almonds. As for the fruit layers (raspberry, peach and rhubarb), they add color and freshness to this irresistible dessert.*

# RHUBARB, PEACH AND RASPBERRY TIRAMISU

**FOR 6 PEOPLE · PREPARATION: 1 3/4 H + OVERNIGHT · COOKING: 5 MIN · REST: 6 H · STORAGE: 3 DAYS**

## INGREDIENTS

***Vegan tiramisu cream:*** ¼ cup (60 ml) blanched almonds, soaked in water overnight • 2 oz. (50 g) firm tofu • 5 oz. (150 g) vegan white chocolate • ½ cup (125 ml) chickpea liquid • 1 tbsp. (15 ml) turbinado (or raw) sugar

***Topping:*** 2 (7-oz. [200 g]) packages ladyfingers (or vegan brioche) • 1 ⅓ cups (325 ml) raspberries (+ 15 to garnish) • 5 peaches (+ 1 for garnish) • about 7 stalks (1 pound [500 g]) rhubarb • 1 bunch white grapes (for garnish) • ½ cup (125 ml) turbinado (or raw) sugar • 1 tbsp. (15 ml) lemon juice • 2 cups (500 ml) green tea, cooled

**1.** Prepare the fruits by first blending the raspberries with 3 tbsp. (45 ml) sugar, and pass the mixture through a sieve to remove the seeds. Peel the peaches, dice them and blend them with the lemon juice and 1 tbsp. (15 ml) sugar. Peel the rhubarb, slice it and cook it with ¼ cup (60 ml) of sugar and a little water; blend the cooked rhubarb.

**2.** To prepare the cream, first rinse the almonds and blend them with the tofu. Melt the white chocolate in a double boiler. Add it to the almond-tofu mixture, and blend again. You should have a thick, uniform paste.

**4.** Beat the chickpea liquid, starting off slowly. Once the liquid begins to turn white, add the sugar, and gradually increase the speed of the mixer. Continue beating until the mixture forms soft peaks. It should be quite firm.

**5.** Using a spatula, fold the whites into the almond-tofu mixture.

**6.** To assemble the tiramisu, start by pouring the tea into a bowl. Dip two or three cookies into the tea, let them soak up some liquid and arrange them in the bottom of one of the glasses. Follow this same procedure with the other 5 glasses. Add a layer of the cream, and smooth out the surface. Add a layer of the raspberry mixture, running the spoon around the inside of the glass. Dip another 2 or 3 cookies into the tea, and place them on top of the raspberry layer. Add another layer of cream, and then follow the same procedure with the peach mixture and then the rhubarb.

**7.** Garnish with the fruit you set aside, and chill for at least 6 hours before serving.

*Fruit leather is fresh fruit that has been dehydrated in a thin sheet that can be cut almost like paper. This recipe is super simple, delicious and aesthetically pleasing, especially when the kiwifruit, mango, apricot, raspberry and blueberry purees are blended together! Fruit leather can be eaten on its own, wrapped around a cake roll or used in a layer cake. No matter how it's enjoyed, fruit leather is a healthy, low-sugar snack.*

# FRUIT LEATHER

FOR 5 PIECES OF FRUIT LEATHER · PREPARATION: 1 H · DRYING: 4–6H · STORAGE: 2 MONTHS

### INGREDIENTS

**Kiwifruit leather:** 2 kiwifruits • ½ small ripe banana • 1 tbsp. (15 ml) lemon juice • 1 ½ tbsp. (22 ml) turbinado (or raw) sugar

**Mango leather:** ½ ripe mango • ½ small ripe banana

**Apricot leather:** 4 fresh (or frozen) apricots • ½ small ripe banana • 1 ½ tbsp. (22 ml) turbinado (or raw) sugar

**Raspberry leather:** 1 ½ cups (375 ml) fresh (or frozen) raspberries • ½ small ripe banana • 1 ½ tbsp. (22 ml) turbinado (or raw) sugar

**Blueberry leather:** ⅔ cup (150 ml) applesauce • ⅓ cup (75 ml) blueberries • 1 tbsp. (15 ml) lemon juice • 1 ½ tbsp. (22 ml) turbinado (or raw) sugar

**1.** Blend the kiwifruits with the banana, lemon juice and sugar. Place about a quarter of the puree aside, and spread the rest on a sheet of parchment paper or non-stick dehydrator sheet.

**2.** Follow the same procedure with the other fruit purees, passing the raspberry puree through a sieve, to remove the seeds. Remember to set aside a quarter of each puree.

**3.** Prepare a multicolored sheet of fruit leather with the purees you set aside (keep the colors separate).

**4.** Dry at 115°F to 120°F (47–50°C) for 4 to 6 hours in a dehydrator or oven, until the fruit purees are completely dry and are easy to remove from the sheets.

**5.** Wrap the fruit leathers in parchment paper and then in plastic wrap to store them.

*Most meringues are tinted with artificial food colorings, which give them unappetizing neon shades. Here, we use natural colorings made with homemade fruit powder! These meringues are cooked until just tender. If you want to make really crunchy meringues, which can be kept longer, go for the Swiss meringue recipe (see page 107).*

# COLORED MERINGUES

FOR 8 PEOPLE · PREPARATION: 45 MIN · COOKING: 40 MIN · STORAGE: 2 WEEKS

**INGREDIENTS**

4 egg whites • 1 splash lemon juice • 1 cup (250 ml) superfine sugar • 1 ½ tsp. (7 ml) turmeric • 1 ½ tsp. (7 ml) beet powder (see page 19) • 1 tsp. (5 ml) black currant powder (see page 19) • 1 tsp. (5 ml) matcha tea

**1.** Start by slowly beating the egg whites with the lemon juice, to help loosen them.

**2.** When they start to foam, gradually add the sugar. Gradually increase the speed of the mixer and beat until you have a thick, shiny meringue.

**3.** Divide the meringue in five and, using a whisk, incorporate one coloring into each batch.

**4.** Preheat oven to 220°F (100°C). Cover three large sheet pans with parchment paper (sticking the paper down with dots of meringue at each corner). Put one color of meringue in a piping bag with a star tip. Make walnut-sized balls on the baking sheets. Follow the same procedure with the remaining colored meringues.

**5.** Bake for 30 to 40 minutes, checking regularly to ensure the meringues keep their pastel shades.

**6.** Cool and store immediately in an airtight container to prevent the meringues from softening.

**Gourmet tip:** you can make two-tone meringues by putting two colors of meringue mixture together in the piping bag.

# FROZEN SNACKS
## AND
# DRINKS

*There are loads of mass-produced ice pops made with water, corn syrup and artificial flavors and colors! No, thanks... In the following recipe, the main ingredients are tasty organic fruits. I've added a hint of turbinado sugar to boost the flavors and a bit of water to thin the mixture out a little — and that's all. Feel free to change the fruits based on the season and the colors!*

# FRUIT ICE POPS

FOR 6 POPS · PREPARATION: 30 MIN · COOKING: 7–8 MIN · REST: 3 H · STORAGE: 6 MONTHS

**INGREDIENTS**

*Green layer:* 1 stalk green rhubarb (fresh or frozen) • 2 ½ tbsp. (37 ml) sugar • ¼ cup (60 ml) water • few mint leaves

*Yellow layer:* ½ mango • 2 tsp. (10 ml) sugar • ¼ cup (60 ml) water

*Orange layer:* 3 apricots (fresh, frozen or canned) • 2 tsp. (10 ml) sugar • ¼ cup (60 ml) water

*Pink layer:* 1 cup raspberries • 2 tsp. (10 ml) sugar • ¼ cup (60 ml) water

*Purple layer:* 1 cup blueberries • 2 tsp. (10 ml) sugar • ¼ cup (60 ml) water

**1.** Peel and slice the rhubarb. Place the rhubarb in a small saucepan, and add the sugar and water. Cover and cook for 7 to 8 minutes. Blend the cooked rhubarb mixture with the mint.

**2.** Blend each of the other fruits separately with the sugar and water. Strain the raspberry mixture to remove the seeds.

**3.** Pour a layer of blueberry puree into 6 ice pop molds (2 to 3 tsp. [20–30 ml]). Chill in the freezer for 30 minutes.

**4.** Take the molds out of the freezer. Insert a wooden stick into each. Pour a layer of raspberry puree over the blueberries, and put the molds back in the freezer.

**5.** Follow the same procedure with the rest of the flavors, following a rainbow color gradient.

**6.** Leave the ice pops in the freezer for at least 3 hours. To unmold them, briefly run them under warm water, and gently pull them out by the stick.

*This recipe is based on a traditional French ice cream called glace Plombières, which is made with kirsch and diced candied fruit. Each scoop is studded with beautifully colored little gems! Hence the idea for this recipe, which features dried fruits and has less sugar and more nutrients — but is just as colorful!*

# DRIED FRUIT ICE CREAM

FOR 8 PEOPLE · REST: 5–10 H + PREPARATION: 20 MIN · STORAGE: 6 MONTHS

## INGREDIENTS

2 ½ cups (625 ml) plain Greek yogurt (or plain soy yogurt) • ¾ cup (175 ml) soy cream • ⅓ cup (75 ml) agave syrup • ½ cup (125 ml) shelled pistachio nuts • 1 or 2 rings dried pineapple • 5 or 6 pieces candied ginger • 5 or 6 slices candied orange • ¼ cup (60 ml) dried cranberries • ¼ cup (60 ml) goji berries

### • WITH AN ICE CREAM MAKER

**1.** At least 8 hours before you're ready to begin, place the bowl of the ice cream maker in the freezer.

**2.** To prepare the ice cream, start by beating the yogurt, soy cream and agave syrup together in a large bowl.

**3.** Chop the pistachio nuts with a chef's knife. Cut the dried pineapple into small pieces with a pair of scissors. Finely chop the candied ginger. Finely dice the candied orange. Mix these fruits together with the cranberries and goji berries.

**4.** Take the bowl out of the freezer and place it in the ice cream maker. Pour the cream into the bowl, and run the machine until the cream solidifies. Add the fruits at the end.

**5.** Scoop the ice cream into an airtight container, garnish the top with fruits (optional) and chill in the freezer for 2 hours before serving.

### • WITHOUT AN ICE CREAM MAKER

**1.** Beat the yogurt, soy cream and agave syrup together in a large bowl.

**2.** Chop the pistachio nuts with a chef's knife. Cut the dried pineapple into small pieces with a pair of scissors. Finely chop the candied ginger. Finely dice the candied orange. Mix these fruits together with the cranberries and goji berries.

**3.** Combine the sweetened cream and fruit together in an airtight container and chill the mixture in the freezer for 45 minutes.

**4.** Take the ice cream mixture out of the freezer, mix well with a fork and put back in the freezer. Follow this same procedure three more times (or more, if necessary), until you have a smooth ice cream.

**5.** Put the ice cream into an airtight container, garnish the top with fruits (optional) and chill in the freezer for 2 hours before serving.

*Simple ice cubes are a thing of the past! Make fruity ice cubes, which have more color and flavor! One option is to simply place fruits in ice cube trays and add water. Alternatively, you can freeze cubes of fruit smoothie. Once they are frozen, add a few fruity cubes to a glass of water, kombucha, iced tea or fruit juice... If you make this recipe when berries are in season, you can store the ice cubes in bulk in a freezer bag and enjoy them all year long.*

# FRUITY ICE CUBES

FOR 2 ICE TRAYS · PREPARATION: 20 MIN · FREEZING: 2 H · STORAGE: 1 YEAR

**INGREDIENTS**

2 kiwifruits • 1 large lemon • one mango "cheek" (see page 91) • ⅓ cup (75 ml) currants • ½ cup (125 ml) raspberries • ⅓ cup (75 ml) blueberries • ½ cup (125 ml) blackberries

**1.** Peel the kiwifruits and slice into quarters. Finely dice one of the quarters. Blend the remaining kiwifruit. Divide the diced kiwifruit between two sections of an ice cube tray. Divide the blended kiwifruit between two sections of a different ice cube tray.

**2.** Wash the other fruits, and follow this same procedure.

**3.** Chill the ice cube trays in the freezer for at least 2 hours.

**Note:** to help make it easier to blend the small quantities of fruit, multiply the quantities indicated in the recipe by three. Consider freezing some for a prepared smoothie for breakfast or a snack. Be careful, however, as smoothies prepared with banana will turn brown when frozen — and even browner when defrosted.

*You'll be amazed at how tasty these fruit-vegetable mixes are! I'm suggesting a few happy unions, but you can certainly improvise. Here's a tip: combine fruits and vegetables of the same color and that have sweet notes. These blends are nearly always successful!*

# FRUIT AND VEGETABLE SMOOTHIES

**FOR 5 SMOOTHIES · PREPARATION: 25 MIN · STORAGE: 2 DAYS**

**INGREDIENTS**

*White smoothie:* 1 rib celery • 1 pear

*Green smoothie:* 1 leaf kale • 2 kiwifruits • 1 small banana

*Yellow smoothie:* 1 small yellow carrot • ½ mango

*Orange smoothie:* 1 small carrot • ½ small tomato • 4 strawberries

*Red smoothie:* ¼ large red pepper • 1 cup (250 ml) red currants

*Pink smoothie:* ½ small beet, raw • 1 cup (250 ml) raspberries

*Purple smoothie:* ¼ cup shredded red cabbage • ½ cup (125 ml) blueberries • ½ medium apple

• Spring water

**1.** Peel and wash the fruits and vegetables.

**2.** Blend each separately in a blender, until they are the consistency of a creamy smoothie. Add a little water to dilute the mixture.

**3.** Using a funnel, pour each smoothie into a small glass bottle.

**4.** Chill and serve.

*This thirst-quenching drink is pleasing to the eye, with its shades of yellow, orange and pink! Rooibo is caffeine free, so it can be drunk by children and adults alike. Children in particular will enjoy this fruity iced tea.*

# FRUITY ROOIBOS ICED TEA

FOR 6 CUPS (1.5 L) · PREPARATION: 20 MIN · COOKING: 5 MIN · RESTING: 1 DAY · STORAGE: 3 DAYS

**INGREDIENTS**

6 cups (1.5 l) water • 3 tbsp. (45 ml) rooibos tea (or 1 bag per cup [250 ml] of water) • 1 orange • 1 lemon • 2 limes • 1 cup (250 ml) raspberries • 1 cup (250 ml) blueberries • 1 vanilla pod • ⅓ cup (75 ml) agave syrup • ice

**1.** Heat up the water to 200°F (95°C). Pour it on the rooibos tea, cover and leave to stand for 5 minutes.

**2.** In the meantime, wash the fruits, including the citrus. Slice the latter. Halve the vanilla pod and scrape the seeds out with the tip of a knife.

**3.** Filter the tea into a large jug and leave to cool. Add the fruits, the halved vanilla pod, the vanilla seeds and the agave syrup. Mix well.

**4.** Chill the tea in the fridge for 1 day, stirring occasionally.

**5.** Serve the tea over ice.

*This cocktail is a crowd pleaser, so why not try the rainbow version? Your guests will be spoilt for choice!*

# MOJITOS

FOR 4 DRINKS · PREPARATION: 20 MIN · STORAGE: NONE

..................................................................................................................................

**INGREDIENTS**

*Green mojito:* 3 tsp. (15 ml) turbinado (or raw) sugar • juice of 1 lime • 1 slice lime • 1 slice kiwifruit
• 1 mint sprig, chopped • 2 fl. oz. (60 ml) white rum

*Yellow mojito:* 3 tsp. (15 ml) turbinado (or raw) sugar • juice from ½ lemon • 1 slice lemon
• flesh from ½ passion fruit • 2 fl. oz. (60 ml) white rum

*Red mojito:* 3 tsp. (15 ml) turbinado (or raw) sugar • juice from 1 blood orange • 1 slice blood orange
• 1 tbsp. (15 ml) red currants • 2 fl. oz. (60 ml) white rum

*Pink mojito:* 3 tsp. (15 ml) turbinado (or raw) sugar • juice from ¼ grapefruit
• 2 or 3 grapefruit wedges or supremes • 4 or 5 raspberries • 2 fl. oz. (60 ml) white rum

• Sparkling water (or club soda) and ice

**1.** Wash the fruit thoroughly (including citrus).

**2.** Take out 4 glasses, and add the sugar to each glass.

**3.** Put the relevant citrus juice and fruits in each glass.

**4.** Add a little sparkling water to each glass, and then add the rum and 3 ice cubes per glass. Top each glass with sparkling water.

**5.** Serve with colored straws, which you can use to help crush the fruits and stir the drink.

# INDEX

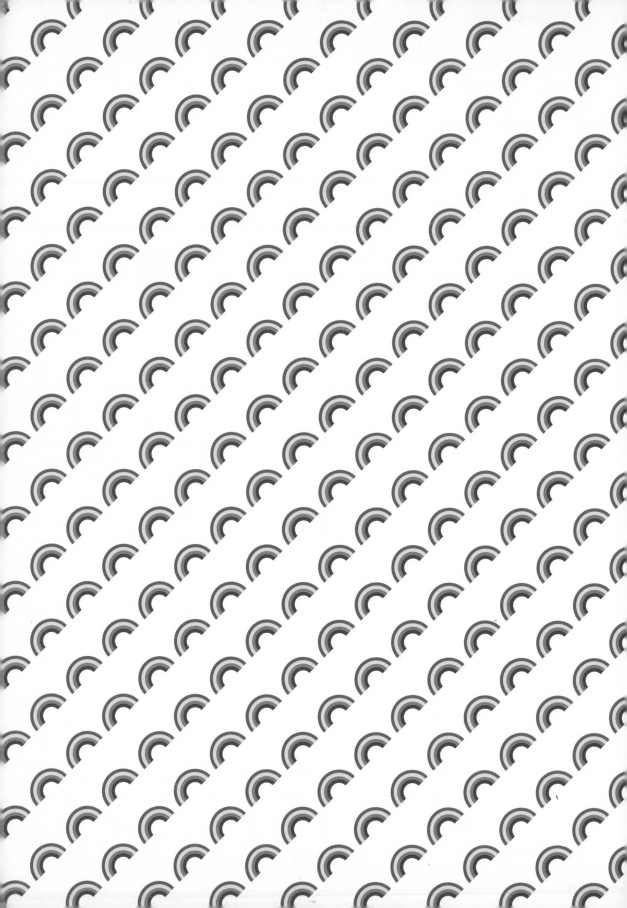